D0848082

Louis Auchincloss

Twayne's United States Authors Series

Warren French, Editor

University College of Swansea, Wales

TUSAS 534

LOUIS AUCHINCLOSS
(1917–   )
Photograph courtesy of Adele Auchincloss

Louis Auchincloss

by David B. Parsell

Furman University

Twayne Publishers
A Division of G.K. Hall & Co. • *Boston*

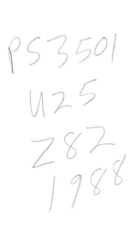

Louis Auchincloss
David B. Parsell

Published by Twayne Publishers
A Division of G.K. Hall & Co.
70 Lincoln Street
Boston, Massachusetts 02111

Copyediting supervised by Michael Sims
Book production by Gabrielle B. McDonald
Book design by Barbara Anderson

Typeset in 11 pt. Garamond
by Compset, Inc., Beverly, Massachusetts

Printed on permanent/durable acid-free paper
and bound in the United States of America

Library of Congress Cataloging-in-Publication Data

Parsell, David B.
   Louis Auchincloss.

   Twayne's United States authors series ; TUSAS 534)
   Bibliography: p.
   Includes index.
   1. Auchincloss, Louis—Criticism and interpretation.
I. Title.   II. Series.
PS3501.U25Z82   1988   813'.54   87-25210
ISBN 0-8057-7516-1

For Sharon, who got there first

Contents

About the Author

A longtime contributor to reference works dealing with French, American, and British authors, David B. Parsell is currently professor of modern languages at Furman University, where he has taught since 1969. A graduate of Hamilton College, with M.A. and Ph.D. degrees from Vanderbilt University, he has also published articles and reviews in the *Comparatist, French Review,* and *Symposium,* and has served since 1978 on the editorial board of the *Comparatist.*

Preface

Although recognized as a "significant" American novelist well before 1960, the year that *The House of Five Talents* would propel him toward the front rank, Louis Auchincloss did not begin to receive serious critical attention until the seventh decade of his life. Clearly the peer, quite possibly the superior, of such older writers as John P. Marquand, John O'Hara, and James Gould Cozzens, all now deceased, Auchincloss, for reasons that remain obscure, has only recently—having lived longer than the first two authors named—begun to receive the recognition that has long been his due.

As a native New York "aristocrat," having "cut his teeth"—and sharpened his vision—on the work of Henry James and Edith Wharton, Auchincloss appears to have suffered, until recently, from the kind of critical backlash that accuses him of trying to make boring people interesting. Interesting, indeed, such people become—when seen through the eyes of a perceptive insider and described in a style trained by decades of voracious reading in a wide range of languages. The United States is fortunate indeed to have had among its practitioners of prose fiction a person who applies to its society and institutions the same level of observation and expository skill in the twentieth century that James and Wharton brought to bear on their own contemporaries. To argue that Auchincloss writes only about New Yorkers, and rich New Yorkers at that, is truly to beg the question: For good or for ill, the manner in which all Americans now live has been shaped by the decisions of "Auchincloss characters," or indeed their prototypes—men and women who have risen to positions of power and prominence either by their own efforts or by those of their ancestors. Auchincloss, throughout his career as a novelist, has endeavored to show the human side of power and, more often than not, succeeded.

The enormous productivity of the author's middle years—both in fiction and in expository prose—has tended, moreover, to hide the true achievement of his strongest novels, written between 1956 and 1966. Among certain observers and reviewers, all Auchincloss characters are now thought to look and act alike, to the point of interchangeability—an allegation hardly borne out by an attentive reading of the novels themselves. An objective assessment of Auchincloss's career as a novelist is thus long overdue, if only to correct the many misconceptions that have arisen in the absence of assembled facts.

Throughout the pages that follow, I have sought to remind—or inform—the reader of Auchincloss's demonstrable accomplishments as storyteller and prose stylist, tracing the evolution of his talent through the early fiction to the four truly great novels of the 1960s, upon which his reputation is most likely to rest. Thereafter, I attempt to isolate and discuss the main themes and concerns of Auchincloss's published fiction, drawing also upon certain later novels as upon selected short stories. Having thus reconstructed the author's fictional universe, I proceed in subsequent chapters to deal with his singular approach to short fiction, his distinguished career as an essayist, and his sustained activity as the author of eminently readable novels. In a brief conclusion I endeavor to point and to share the lessons that I myself have learned in preparing this book, the better to speed Auchincloss's deserved recognition as a major American novelist. Since Auchincloss's fiction is available in so many various editions, page references are not supplied for quotations from the works.

I should like here to recognize Mr. Auchincloss's generous assistance in providing materials and information as needed. It is perhaps worth noting, however, that he has not sought to intrude upon the work-in-progress and that I, in turn, have endeavored throughout to let his work speak for itself, without benefit of the author's own opinions except, as with *A Writer's Capital,* in published form. I should like also to acknowledge my gratitude to Ms. Athenaide Dallett of the Twayne editorial staff and my field editor, Professor Warren French, for their keen interest in the project.

To Furman University, I am grateful for a half-year sabbatical leave that enabled me to complete the manuscript, and for the secretarial skills of Mesdames Linda Ray and Carolyn Sims. I should also like to thank my daughter Marty and son Jay for their understanding as the project claimed an increasing share of their father's time and attention. Finally, I should like to express special thanks to my wife, Sharon Youngblood Parsell, who, knowing my abiding interest in the works of Marquand and O'Hara, suggested nearly twenty years ago that I try reading *The Embezzler* and *The Rector of Justin.* More recently, Sharon's sustained interest in this project and its subject has been a steady source of encouragement—even as we tend to disagree on the relative merits of particular Auchincloss novels. Again many thanks to all.

David B. Parsell

Furman University

Chronology

1960 *The House of Five Talents*. Birth of Blake Leay Auchincloss.

1961 *Reflections of a Jacobite*, collected essays.

1962 *Portrait in Brownstone. Edith Wharton* (essay).

1963 *Powers of Attorney* (short stories). Birth of Andrew Sloane Auchincloss.

1964 *The Rector of Justin. Ellen Glasgow* (essay).

1965 *Pioneers and Caretakers* (literary criticism).

1966 *The Embezzler*.

1967 *Tales of Manhattan*.

1968 *A World of Profit*.

1969 *Motiveless Malignity* (literary criticism).

1970 *Second Chance* (short stories).

1971 *Henry Adams* and *Edith Wharton, A Woman in Her Time* (essays).

1972 *I Come as a Thief. Richelieu* (illustrated essay).

1974 *The Partners* (linked short fictions published as a novel). *A Writer's Capital* (autobiographical essay).

1975 *Reading Henry James* (literary criticism).

1976 *The Winthrop Covenant*.

1977 *The Dark Lady*.

1978 *The Country Cousin*.

1979 *Life, Law and Letters* (collected essays and reviews).

1980 *The House of the Prophet*.

1981 *The Cat and the King*.

1982 *Watchfires*.

1983 *Exit Lady Masham. Narcissa and Other Fables*.

1984 *The Book Class. False Dawn* (essays).

1985 *Honorable Men*.

1986 *Diary of a Yuppie*. Retires from Hawkins, Delafield and Wood at end of year.

1987 *Skinny Island* (short stories).

Chapter One

Auchincloss and the American Novel of Manners after World War II

In 1960, on the threshold of his own maturity as a novelist, Louis Auchincloss published in the *Nation* an article rather modestly titled "Marquand and O'Hara: The Novel of Manners."[1] If the title was modest, the article itself was not, implying that the authors named had failed to breathe life into a dying convention that, in the United States at least, had reached its high-water mark no less than fifty years earlier with the works of Henry James and Edith Wharton. No small part of the problem, suggested Auchincloss, was that American society had by the middle of the twentieth century become so "classless" that the would-be novelist of manners, be he Marquand or O'Hara, was reduced to inventing stratifications instead of merely observing them.

Concentrating in particular upon Marquand's *Point of No Return* (1949) and O'Hara's very first novel, *Appointment in Samarra* (1934), Auchincloss sees the convention shading away from the social toward the psychological, away from the analysis of manners toward the minute description of individual mannerisms: Marquand's Charles Gray, for example, is hampered less by his social environment than by his own misconceptions of that environment; similarly, the spectacular suicide of O'Hara's Julian English would seem, in the final analysis, to derive less from external pressures than from internal ones. In the work of both writers, meanwhile, rivalries spring up not among classes but rather among cliques operating at roughly the same social level. Perhaps, Auchincloss suggests, the novel of manners has come to an impasse for want of direction or material.

As it happens, Auchincloss was by no means the first would-be novelist of manners in America to call the convention into serious question. As James Tuttleton points out in *The Novel of Manners in America* (1972), such earlier practitioners as James Fenimore Cooper and even Henry James had viewed the proposition as a possible contradiction in terms; presumably, the "land of the free" would seem at first glance an unlikely breeding ground for a novelistic convention so deeply rooted in the fertile soil of feudal and postfeudal Europe. As both Cooper and James would soon learn, however, social mobility is no proof against discrimination or exclusion, and stratification would continue to assert itself regardless of location or official policy. As Auchincloss himself had already demonstrated in his earliest novels, stratifications continued to exist, well into the postwar era; what apparently bothered him most about O'Hara and Marquand was less their choice of subject matter than their evident ignorance, or at least disregard, of the "tradition" to which they were perhaps inadvertently contributing.

It is a matter of record that, of the three major writers active in the convention after World War II, Auchincloss was most familiar with the "tradition" brought close to perfection by James and Wharton, later embellished by F. Scott Fitzgerald in *The Great Gatsby*. To be sure, both Marquand and O'Hara had approached the convention more or less by accident; as the various biographers of both men make clear, both were highly observant "outsiders" who had suffered, or believed that they had suffered, serious rebuffs from those "on the inside" who "had gone to the right schools." In general, Marquand and O'Hara tended to write from the breadth of what they saw through the depth of what they felt, little mindful of any "tradition" from which they might derive, or to which they might have been contributing. Auchincloss, by contrast, was and is very much the "insider" by dint of birth and schooling; by the time he turned to the writing of fiction, moreover, he was already well versed in the "tradition," including even the lesser-known British and Continental models. His expectations of O'Hara and Marquand, therefore, might well have exceeded those authors' own avowed intentions. Besides, Auchincloss's own published fiction, though noteworthy, had by 1960 given little promise of the richness that would follow soon thereafter, richness that would doubtless have lent greater authority to his criticism of two older contemporaries whose works were then held in fairly high esteem. As it happened, Marquand had died, at age sixty-six, some six months before the article appeared; O'Hara, however, would take continued offense for the remaining decade until his own death at sixty-five, denigrating Auchincloss as an aristocratic interloper upon territory that he, John O'Hara, had long since staked out as his own.

By 1980, twenty years after the death of Marquand and ten years after that of O'Hara, the novel of manners appeared all but obsolete.

Marquand's novels, in particular, had begun to show their age very quickly, and O'Hara's had lost ground in favor of the incisive, memorable shorter pieces that had appeared, in book form, nearly every Thanksgiving for the last ten years of his life. Auchincloss, vigorously active in his sixties, stood virtually alone and unchallenged as a practitioner of the convention; *The House of the Prophet,* published in 1980, invited comparison with such of his acclaimed earlier works as *The Rector of Justin* (1964) and *The Embezzler* (1966). Few other authors, meanwhile, had endeavored to write novels of manners, although elements of the convention were still to be found, albeit somewhat dispersed, in a number of critically acclaimed mainstream novels. By 1986, Auchincloss had published five additional novels, three of them set a hundred or more years in the past, and a well-received collection of short stories. In a sense, the "fate" of the novel of manners in America remained as undecided as Auchincloss had found it a quarter century before, with the bulk of his own fiction still awaiting serious evaluation.

James Tuttleton, who in 1972 viewed Auchincloss as the most recent exemplar of a tradition extending from Cooper, William Dean Howells, and James through the work of Edith Wharton, Sinclair Lewis, and Fitzgerald, including James Gould Cozzens along with Marquand and O'Hara, tends to agree with Auchincloss's own earlier assessment concerning the novel of manners. Beginning with Marquand and O'Hara, he suggests, the novel of manners has dealt increasingly with psychological concerns, a tendency inherent in the works of Auchincloss himself. Tuttleton, in fact, goes even so far as to exclude from the convention such novels as *The Rector of Justin* and *A World of Profit,* more properly viewed, he suggests, as novels of "character"; the same could doubtless be said of *The House of the Prophet.* Still, the prevailing social structure and texture of *all* Auchincloss's novels demand that they be viewed, at least initially, with relation to the tradition of which Auchincloss is at once practitioner, student, and critic.

The term "novel of manners," together with the concept to which it refers, has been in currency for at least two centuries, yet it continues to elude close definition. Tuttleton, in describing the nature and scope of his inquiry, works primarily within a definition set forth by Lionel Trilling in an essay published shortly after World War II:

What I understand by manners, then, is a culture's hum and buzz of implication. I mean the whole evanescent context in which its explicit statements are made. It is that part of a culture which is made up of half-uttered or unutterable expressions of value. They are hinted at by small actions. Sometimes by the arts of dress or decoration, sometimes by tone, gesture, emphasis, or rhythm, sometimes by the words that are used with a special frequency or a special meaning. They are the things that separate them from the people of another culture. They make the part of a culture which is not art, or religion, or morals, or politics, and yet it relates to all these highly formulated departments of culture. It is modified by them; it modifies them; it is generated by them; it generates them. In this part of culture assumption rules, which is often so much stronger than reason.[2]

Thus formulated, Trilling's definition affords Tuttleton ample room for the inclusion of such character-intensive narratives as those of Auchincloss, Fitzgerald, O'Hara, and Marquand. The question is largely one of balance, of proportion, of the degree to which social structures and concerns relate to the development of character; in the novel of manners per se, individual characters define themselves according to the way they function, or attempt to function, within a given framework of custom and convention. Individual motivations aside, such characters as Jay Gatsby, Nick Carraway, Julian English, and Charley Gray ultimately reveal, express, discover or fail to discover themselves through their responses to the "hum and buzz of implication" going on around them. The psychological novel, by contrast, deals less with social interaction than with the character's inner development, as in John Updike's Rabbit Angstrom novels. Elsewhere, as with Auchincloss's strongest novels of the 1960s, it is somewhat difficult to draw the line; arguably, however, even *The Rector of Justin* fits more or less neatly within the limits of Trilling's proposed definition: For good or for ill, the enigmatic Francis Prescott not only has received, but also helps to perpetuate and even to create the unspoken assumptions of his society. It is this concern with interactive structure that locates Auchincloss squarely within the tradition, even as his probing analysis and delineation of character would relate him also to his post-Freudian contemporaries outside it.

Regardless of the difference between Auchincloss's works and those of the two writers whom he chose to discuss in the *Nation*, he is by any standard their logical, if not their chosen, successor. Like it or not, his featured characters and the problems that they face inevitably recall those to be encountered in the novels of O'Hara and Marquand; what is more, Auchincloss, after spending World War II as a naval officer on active duty, was able to deal with the war and its social repercussions in a more authentic manner than the two older writers, who had been too old to serve and had seen action only as correspondents. His work must thus be seen as continuing Marquand and O'Hara's fictional analysis of the interwar years through and beyond the upheavals wrought by Pearl Harbor and Hiroshima. Close kin, despite their early advantages, to Julian English and Charley Gray, such early Auchincloss protagonists as Michael Farish, Timothy Colt, and Reese Parmelee face the additional challenges of the war itself and of inevitable postwar changes in the structure of their jobs and marriages. Like Julian English, Michael Farish will opt for suicide when drunk, having burnt behind him most of the bridges that he can perceive even when sober; the others will survive, albeit in considerably altered states. The territory surveyed, however, remains familiar to readers acquainted with the work of O'Hara and Marquand.

In 1960, shortly before his article on Marquand and O'Hara appeared in the *Nation,* Auchincloss published *The House of Five Talents,* generally acknowledged to be his finest, if least "typical" novel thus far, and the one that would herald the arrival of his full maturity as a novelist. Unlike his earlier tales, recounted in the relatively affectless third-person narrative favored by O'Hara, *The House of Five Talents* is told in the first person by a narrator as unlike the author as possible, a seventy-five-year-old spinster presumably writing her memoirs during the summer of 1948. As Auchincloss would later recall, he had decided at last "to write the novel that everyone thought I had been writing," in which the characters are primarily "shaped" by their money. Miss Augusta Millinder, a most informed yet credible and entertaining narrator, is memorable also as a character in her own right, born and bred to develop keen powers of observation and a strong, if acquired, taste for meddling. Marquand, in his earliest novels, had employed first-person narration with varying degrees of success, but Auchincloss's creation of "Miss Gussie" truly broke new ground in the postwar novel of manners as well as in his own career, performing a tour de force that he would later equal more than once, but probably never surpass.

Marquand had written no new novels after 1958, and after his death in 1960 only O'Hara remained to practice his craft, often in open defiance of Auchincloss's increasing and increasingly recognized accomplishments. After 1960, O'Hara would publish only five more novels of manners during his lifetime, the bulk of his prodigious activity going into generally well written short fiction set mainly in the 1920s, the period of his own youth and early maturity. Such volumes as *Ourselves To Know* (1960), *Elizabeth Appleton* (1963), and *The Lockwood Concern* (1965) added little to the existing O'Hara novelistic canon, leaving the field more or less open to Auchincloss's steadily developing skill and virtuosity in *Portrait in Brownstone* (1962), *The Rector of Justin* (1964), and *The Embezzler* (1966). *The Rector of Justin,* in particular, brought to Auchincloss a degree of recognition and even celebrity that had previously eluded him, assuring at least that his subsequent novels would be watched very closely indeed.

Initially praised for the author's skill in presenting his title character, the Reverend Francis Prescott of Justin Martyr Academy, *The Rector of Justin* ultimately attracted wide notice and readership because in it Auchincloss tackled, more skillfully and forthrightly than had been done before, the paradoxical existence in democratic America of an elitist superstructure modeled upon the British system of so-called public schools. Ironically, the many-sided but single-minded Prescott goes to his grave deploring the very inequalities that he and his school have helped to foster and perpetuate, against his will and indeed without his even noticing. Although Auchincloss's earlier protagonists, like the author himself, bore to a man the indelible stamp of elite preparatory school, *The Rector of Justin* went farther and deeper than any of his previous works in assessing the role of such schools in the shaping of American society after the Civil War. The novel was notable also for the author's skillful use of multiple viewpoint and voice, a technique that Auchincloss first used in *Portrait in Brownstone* and to which he would return in *The Embezzler.* If such a technique, as Tuttleton has noted, enhances the simplicity of the character Prescott,[3] it also displays the author's capacity to examine his subject, as indeed his society, from a multiplicity of angles and viewpoints.

The Rector of Justin was still the focus of considerable critical and popular attention when Auchincloss published *The Embezzler,* a novel that would keep his name and work in the public eye for a few years longer. Although perhaps less ambitious than his study of the fictional Francis Prescott, Auchincloss's analysis of the public disgrace of Wall Street during the Depression and its aftermath displayed the same technical skill as the earlier novel; as in *The Rector of Justin,* multiple viewpoints serve both to inform and to disorient the reader. Into the person of Guy Prime, title character and occasional narrator, Auchincloss manages to combine the crime of a known historical figure with the personality and background of a wholly fictional character; incidentally, both Guy Prime and his eventual antagonist Rex Geer, son of a New England parson, owe much to the characters and settings of Marquand. At the same time, however, they derive also from Auchincloss's own maturing vision, expressed and developed most clearly in *The House of Five Talents* and *Portrait in Brownstone*. Owing in no small measure to the complexity of the major characters, *The Embezzler* manages to breathe credible life into what might otherwise seem a dull, if crucial moment in recent American history.

Only with the publication of Auchincloss's subsequent novel, *A World of Profit* (1968), did the particular strengths and weaknesses of his talent begin to come into full focus. As indicated by his choice of a parvenu named Jay as featured character, Auchincloss in *A World of Profit* appears at times to be attempting a rewrite of *The Great Gatsby* for the 1960s, with the basic difference that it is not the parvenu who dies. Although well written in Auchincloss's polished, reflective style, *A World of Profit* ultimately fails as a novel, in part through the author's eventual inability to deal with the contemporary period. Ironically, the strongest passages in *A World of Profit* are those recalling the characters' childhood and adolescence some thirty years earlier.

Although Auchincloss was originally hailed as the first postwar novelist of manners, the novels published after 1970 tended increasingly to classify him as a chronicler of the 1930s, much as O'Hara in his later years was identified with the 1920s. Seen in the reflected light of his later efforts, even such earlier accomplishments as *The Rector of Justin* and *The Embezzler* appeared to lose some of their luster, diminished by comparison with such later chronicles as *The Dark Lady* (1977) and *The Country Cousin* (1978). Of those novels written after 1970, the strongest and most memorable appear to be *The House of the Prophet* (1980), loosely but frankly based on the life of the columnist Walter Lippmann, and *Watchfires* (1982), a novel not unlike *The Embezzler* but set at the time of the Civil War. By the mid-1980s, Auchincloss's reputation appeared to be endangered primarily by his astonishing productivity. Virtually without competition as a novelist of manners, Auchincloss in his sixties continued to turn out long fiction at the approximate rate of one novel per year, together with nonfiction and collected short fiction; for a number of critics and readers, the sheer bulk of his published output tended to obscure his more significant accomplishments. It is worth noting, however, that several volumes of his short fiction, including *Tales of Manhattan* (1967), *Second Chance*

(1970), *The Partners* (1974), and *Narcissa and Other Fables* (1983), continued to draw generally favorable reviews, owing in part to Auchincloss's sustained experimentation with a hybrid form located somewhere between the short story and the novel. Arguably, Auchincloss's generally successful exploration of the boundaries (if any) between two forms ranks among his greater accomplishments.

Chapter Two
A Writer's Capital

Like John P. Marquand and John O'Hara, his immediate predecessors as American novelists and chroniclers of manners, Louis Auchincloss was born to privilege, and to the fruits of material success. He was never, however, subjected to the sudden, precipitous decline in family fortunes that marked the lives and careers of both O'Hara and Marquand from adolescence. A member of the establishment since birth, Auchincloss has, perhaps enviably, managed to hold his place in it for life, having attended the "right" schools before joining its active ranks as an attorney practicing on Wall Street. Arguably, the lack of adversity or incident in his life might well have blunted his skills as a satirist; on the other hand, his work is notably and at times refreshingly free of the blinding social resentment that often impairs the observations of O'Hara and Marquand.

In 1974, recalling the dictum that "A writer's childhood is his entire capital," Auchincloss undertook to write a brief, selective memoir covering roughly the first thirty years of his life, with occasional reference to works written much later. The apparent aim of *A Writer's Capital* is to explore and, in part, to explain the relationship of the author's works to his life, incidentally exploring also his double vocation as lawyer and writer. Like the pronouncements of any other author, those in *A Writer's Capital* might best be approached with caution and some skepticism; on balance, however, the volume emerges as a generally straightforward, occasionally rueful account of the author's background and experience, notable also for its acknowledgment of literary influences.

Louis Stanton Auchincloss was born 27 September 1917 at Lawrence, Long Island, New York, the third of four children and the second of three sons. His father, Joseph Howland Auchincloss (1886–1968), was himself a Wall Street lawyer, eventually associated with the firm best known as "Davis, Polk," founded by John W. Davis, the 1924 Democratic nominee for the U. S. presidency. Louis's mother, the former Priscilla Stanton, was by her famous son's recollection a woman of many interests and talents, bound nonetheless by an unwritten code of her generation that forbade development of career interests apart from those of her husband. Early in *A Writer's Capital* Auchincloss attempts to set straight the record concerning his family's affluence and its sources:

There never was an Auchincloss fortune. Some New York families have a "robber baron" founder, as others have a colonial governor, and Roman ones a pope. But each generation of Auchincloss men made or married its own money. My father, one of five children with living parents, was able at twenty-five to marry an unendowed girl, but only by virtue of an allowance from his father of five thousand dollars a year and the loan by his mother-in-law of a floor of her house at 30 West 49th Street. Life was easier then—for some. Seven years later, in 1918, when my mother took me, an infant, and my older brother and sister to Louisville, where Father was in officers' training camp, four Irish maids went with her, and nobody suggested that this was an excessive luxury for a young lawyer's wife. [1]

The tone of the above excerpt, generally indicative of that to be found throughout *A Writer's Capital,* displays a curious admixture of blindness and insight, together with the reflective irony that also characterizes the author's mature creative work. Throughout his career as a novelist Auchincloss has often had occasion to defend his privileged background, often against fellow writers who grew to maturity under far less favorable circumstances. His response, characteristically, has been somewhat ambivalent, tending to play down the privileges afforded by wealth while refusing to abandon them, even in conjecture. To Hemingway and Fitzgerald alike, Auchincloss might well reply that the rich are indeed no different from anyone else, despite the fact that they have more money.

As Auchincloss is quick to point out from the opening pages onward, his Scottish ancestors had little in their favor save for their industry, which found its expression in the wool trade. The author's immigrant paternal ancestor Hugh, arriving in New York in 1803 aboard a ship "appropriately named the *Factor,*" proceeded to establish a highly successful American branch of the family textile business, along with the beginnings of a family, which, by the author's own estimate, would continue to produce an astonishingly large proportion of male, hence name-perpetuating descendants. It is thus possible to conclude that the Auchinclosses, although relatively new to the New World, lost little time in making their industrious presence felt through sheer force of numbers.

In all fairness to Auchincloss the author, it is perhaps worthwhile to note that, by most acceptable social standards of the nineteenth century, his ancestors were no doubt less distinguished than those of Marquand, descended from the New England Fullers, if somewhat more so than those of O'Hara, similarly distinguished by their industry yet shunned due to the then-prevalent prejudice against the Irish. Such advantages as Auchincloss might have enjoyed over his erstwhile competitors are therefore reduced to little more than sheer luck; at birth and during early childhood, his circumstances were approximately equal to those enjoyed by O'Hara as "the Doctor's son" and by Marquand as the grandson of the John Phillips Marquand for whom he was named. Ironically, both older authors were perceived, at least during their lifetimes, as owing their literary careers to an early experience of "expulsion from Paradise" that prevented Marquand from going to private preparatory school and O'Hara from attending college: Marquand, in his fiction both long and short, dealt often with "prep" schools, and O'Hara with the intricacies of college and fraternity life; Auchincloss, a product of both Groton and Yale, also deals with such institutions in his fiction, often with a strong satirical edge to his exposition. In dealing with Auchincloss's fiction, it is therefore important not to accord undue weight to his "patrician" status with relation to his two immediate predecessors, but rather to seek the common ground that he shares with the two older novelists.

As soon as he reached school age, the young Louis Auchincloss was sent to the Bovee School for Boys, a nonboarding establishment then in its declining years. The school's founder, Miss Kate Bovee, died during the first year of Louis's attendance there, leaving the school to her sister Eleanor who, by Auchincloss's account, ran it rather eccentrically and erratically before selling out some five years later. Unlike many similar institutions, however, Bovee School at least admitted students regardless of creed; Auchincloss recalls that there were a number of Jewish students in his class, including the later-famous actors Mel Ferrer and Efrem Zimbalist, Jr. All in all, the experience appears to have done more good than harm, and by the time Bovee closed its doors in 1929 the future novelist was old enough to enroll at Groton, following in the footsteps of his father and elder brother.

By the time he enrolled at Groton, the Massachusetts preparatory school had already acquired the legendary reputation that it has never really lost, not even in the more egalitarian latter half of the twentieth century. For good or for ill, Groton still looms large as *the* New England preparatory school, training ground of presidents, diplomats, and leaders of men. During Auchincloss's time and for some time thereafter, the school was still administered firsthand by its founder, the Reverend Endicott Peabody, known as "the Rector." In *A Writer's Capital* Auchincloss takes considerable pains to explain that the title character of *The Rector of Justin* is modeled not upon Peabody but upon another of his erstwhile heroes, the eminent jurist Learned Hand (1872–1956); as he shows through a detailed comparison of Francis Prescott of Justin and his real-life counterpart of Groton, Peabody was a man of action rather than of thought, a characteristic shared by Judge Hand and the fictional Prescott. Notwithstanding, Peabody's dominance of his school and lifelong influence over its alumni are accurately reflected in the novel, as is the general outline of the real-life rector's beliefs. In any case, Auchincloss's years at Groton provided most of the decisive influences upon his future life and career, including the love of literature that would lead to his vocation as a writer.

Malcolm Strachan, perhaps the strongest and most influential of his mentors, did not join the school's faculty until fairly late in Auchincloss's stay at Groton, by which time the future author had, by his own admission, a great deal to unlearn. Strachan, recalled and described by his disciple as an enthusiastic reader rather than a "critic," set little store by the high grades that were by then Auchincloss's principal goal. Instead he invited his pupils to savor the simple delights of literature accepted on its own merits. As Auchincloss freely admits, Strachan's salutary example did not truly take effect upon him until some time later, during his years at Yale and thereafter; in any case, the first seeds had been planted.

Auchincloss entered Yale from Groton in 1935, having briefly entertained the fantasy of completing his education in France, at the Université de Grenoble. It was during his Yale years that he deepened his acquaintance with the masterpieces of world literature, with the help of such acknowledged master teachers as Samuel Hemingway, Chauncey Tinker, and Joseph Seronde; it was also during this period that he sharpened his skills as a social observer and would-be satirist, frequenting perhaps more than his share of debutante parties for "the spectacle":

I collected parties. I would go to one where I knew nobody at all, simply because it was given in a house or club that I wanted to see or because something interested me about my host or hostess. I was fascinated by New York families and loved to push back into the past for the origin of each. I became something of a joke for my cultivation of the ancient, and I remembered being seated, at a dinner before the Tuxedo Ball, at a tiny table with old Mrs. Tilford, its founder. And at a coming-out party at The Breakers, in Newport, I spent a large part of my evening talking to an elderly man who recalled a dance given in that same hall by Vanderbilts at the turn of the century when footmen in maroon livery had lined the whole of the great marble stairway. (*WC*, 71)

Under the double influence of his reading and his observations, Auchincloss soon undertook to write his own novel of manners, featuring characters who would not reenter his fiction until some forty-five years later, with *Narcissa and Other Fables* (1983), and then in somewhat altered form. When the manuscript was rejected, though with some encouragement, Auchincloss, hardly surprised, chose to interpret the publisher's (Scribner's) decision as an omen of sorts, indicating that he should follow his father into the more serious study and practice of law, and with all possible haste. Deciding to curtail his Yale education after three years, he actively sought the best law school that would accept him without benefit of a bachelor's degree, and in the fall of 1938 began his legal studies at the University of Virginia.

As Auchincloss recalls in *A Writer's Capital* and later in the novel *Honorable Men* (1985), the University of Virginia, and particularly its law school, had become something of a haven for the privileged and well derived, many of whom, unlike himself, were already married and, moreover, stood in line to inherit family business interests. Although academic and professional standards at the school remained uncommonly high then as now, the privileged members of the student body had managed to bring a large part of their life-style with them, often but not always including domestic servants, and the general atmosphere resembled that of a distinguished country club. Notwithstanding, Auchincloss applied himself to his studies with the same single-minded determination that had marked his last years at Groton. Having grimly determined neither to read nor to write fiction while enrolled in law school, he remained true to his self-given word, soon warming to the study of law and legal prose, and rising to positions of increasing responsibility on the editorial board of the *Law Review*.

Still, the ghost of Auchincloss's earlier aspirations was not entirely laid. During the summer of 1938, before leaving for Charlottesville, he had written and discarded half of a second novel, and in *A Writer's*

Capital he vividly recalls his emotions upon driving through Baltimore en route to Virginia, on the very day of novelist Thomas Wolfe's untimely death in that city. In the manner of a resolute, recovering addict, he saw fiction as a temptation to be avoided at all costs: Encouraged by a family friend to call on the Princess Pierre Troubetzkoy, who under her maiden name of Amélie Rives had achieved some measure of fame as a novelist, Auchincloss deliberately delayed the meeting until late fall, by which time he felt sufficiently secure in the law to resist the possible risk of contagion. In time, the freshman law student and the septuagenarian writer would become close friends, yet Auchincloss doggedly refused Mme Troubetzkoy's requests to show her samples of his prose; after all, such samples as remained were safely under lock and key in his parents' New York apartment. Later, he would regret that Amélie Rives, who died in 1945 at eighty-two, did not live long enough to witness the success of his earliest novels.

Impulsive as it may have seemed at the time, Auchincloss's decision to begin law school without waiting to graduate from Yale turned out to have been a wise choice, allowing him to complete his studies and actually to practice his profession for several months before his country's entry into World War II in December 1941. In June of that year he was hired by the prestigious Wall Street firm of Sullivan and Cromwell, where he had worked as a student clerk or "summer boarder" during his vacation the previous year. After the inevitable disruption of military service, he was thus doubly fortunate: His studies were behind him, and a secure job awaited his return.

Auchincloss's service as an officer in the U.S. Navy, duly reflected in his early novels and short fiction, took him from initial posting in the Canal Zone to eventual action in both Atlantic and Pacific theaters. The Canal Zone, an incongruous American outpost little touched by the war, provided the observant young officer with ample material for his later satires of the military bureaucracy and its after-hours social life, particularly in *The Indifferent Children* (1947). Auchincloss's tour of duty in England prior to the D-day invasion would furnish part of the background for *Venus in Sparta,* and his later service in the Pacific inspired a number of the short pieces collected in *The Romantic Egoists.* Auchincloss did not, however, attempt to commit his observations to paper at the time; what he did instead, in such spare time as was available to him, was to catch up on the serious reading that had somehow eluded him during his pursuit of high academic distinction at Groton and at Yale. Thus did he familiarize himself, as a pleasure-hungry reader, with the complete works of authors as diverse as Shakespeare, Gibbon, Trollope, Daudet, Bourget, James, and Wharton. It was not until the very end of the war, when he was stationed in the South Pacific, that he began to plan and write *The Indifferent Children,* combining his memories of the Canal Zone with equally distant memories of the characters who had populated his two earlier attempts at long fiction.

Upon returning to civilian life, Auchincloss took a brief vacation to finish the novel-in-progress before resuming work at Sullivan and Cromwell. Still unmarried as he approached the age of thirty, he found himself more than ever torn between his two apparently conflicting "vocations," literature and the law; although very much at home in legal practice and in the life of a large Manhattan law firm with its reassuring structures and patterns ("a sort of benevolent Navy"), Auchincloss felt little ambition for an eventual partnership, with its attendant seniority and responsibilities. "I was Peter Pan," he recalls wryly, adding that he felt little common bond with his upwardly mobile contemporaries at Sullivan and Cromwell, most of whom had families to support.

The Indifferent Children, meanwhile, had fared better than Auchincloss might have expected; the young lawyer continued to write in his spare time, producing both the novel *Sybil* (1951) and the short stories that would comprise *The Injustice Collectors.* At one point, recalling an earlier ambition, Auchincloss inquired at Yale about the feasibility of completing a Ph.D. in English as preparation for an academic career. Robert French, one of his former professors, was at first encouraging, yet quickly dissuaded him with the words, "You have trained yourself to one noble profession, and you are already cheating on it. What extraordinary compulsion makes you wish to train yourself to another in order to do the same thing?" Notwithstanding, Auchincloss remained dissatisfied. "The situation ultimately became impossible," he relates, adding, "I had to find out, once and for all, what I was" (*WC,* 118–19). Late in 1951, accepting his father's generous offer of financial support, he at last resigned from Sullivan and Cromwell in order to devote all his time and energy to his writing.

Paradoxically, although perhaps not surprisingly, Auchincloss's extended furlough from the law did little to improve either his spirits or his writing, and after two years he was back on Wall Street in search of a job, barred by company policy from returning to Sullivan and Cromwell once he had resigned. By his own admission the novels and stories produced during his leave of absence differed little "in quantity or quality" from those written earlier, during evenings and weekends "borrowed" from Wall Street; indeed, the only lasting benefit that Auchincloss appears to have gained from his leave was the experience of psychoanalysis, a temporal luxury he could never have afforded while juggling the double careers of novelist and lawyer. It is likely that his edifying sessions with Dr. John Cotton served to hone his developing skills by revisiting the past from varying perspectives. In any case, Auchincloss the novelist would go on to feature psychoanalysis and its practitioners in several of his narratives, invariably under a favorable and sympathetic light.

Returning to Wall Street in 1954 with the firm of Hawkins, Delafield and Wood, Auchincloss resumed his dual careers with new dedication and fresh energy, soon embarking on the richest and most productive phase of his writing career. In 1957, not long before his fortieth birthday, he married the former Adele Lawrence, a Rockefeller descendant some dozen years his junior who would eventually bear him three sons; in 1958 he was elevated to full partnership in Hawkins, Delafield and Wood. Meanwhile, he became increasingly well known as the author of three strong, well-received novels, *The Great World and Timothy Colt* (1956), *Venus in Sparta* (1958), and *Pursuit of the Prodigal* (1959). Yet unforeseen were the major successes of the 1960s that would assure popular as well as critical success for the author of *The Rector of Justin,* with frequent interviews printed in such mass-market magazines as *Life, Time,* and *People.*

The account furnished in *A Writer's Capital* ends with the author's return to Wall Street, stopping short of his marriage and the blossoming of his dual careers. Its stated aim, after all, was to show how and why Auchincloss became a writer, not to tell what happened after he became one. To a large extent, as the scope of the book implies, Auchincloss's life after age forty has been inextricably merged with the substance of his published works; indeed, in the well-ordered life that he eventually chose for himself, his books constitute perhaps the only notable "incident."

Chapter Three

Toward a Certain Style

Auchincloss arrived gradually at his mature narrative expression, although not nearly so slowly as the general reader might imagine. His
first published novel, *The Indifferent Children,* is generally mature and
well developed, clearly announcing the young author's deliberate
choice of form and subject matter. Even more mature are the short
fictions written around the same time, published in book form during
1950 as *The Injustice Collectors. Sybil* (1951) and *A Law for the Lion*
(1953), written and published during Auchincloss's two-year "vacation" from the law, clearly show the author's increasing interest in
women as characters, announcing the theme of female self-discovery
that would loom large in his later novels. Between 1956 and 1959
Auchincloss returned his attention to the male of the species with three
strong novels that invited comparison with the best recent works of
O'Hara and Marquand: *The Great World and Timothy Colt* (1956), expanded from a short story included in *The Romantic Egoists,* traces the
life and career of a young attorney undone by his own quixotic idealism; *Venus in Sparta,* published in 1958, portrays the personal and
professional background of a banker's suicide, and *Pursuit of the Prodigal*
(1959) chronicles a well-derived lawyer's vain efforts to turn his back
upon the social forces that helped to produce him. The best novels of
this period, although generally strong and promising, nonetheless lack
the individual stamp of greatness or near-greatness that would mark
the author's major efforts of the 1960s.

The Indifferent Children

A first novel is not to be undertaken lightly, and Auchincloss is
surely not the first fledgling writer to have wondered whether his initial venture into long fiction would indeed best represent him in that
category. Perhaps fortunately, the matter was soon taken out of his
hands by Charles Scribner's Sons, whose editors rejected that first manuscript while encouraging him to send them his "next." As noted in
chapter 2, the planned second novel was never completed, although

characters from both manuscripts eventually found their way into Auchincloss's third effort, published in 1947 by Prentice-Hall as *The Indifferent Children*. Even then, the question arose once again: Was *The Indifferent Children* indeed a wise choice of "first novel," the auspicious start to a promising literary career? The author's mother, for one, thought otherwise, Once the manuscript was accepted for publication, Priscilla Auchincloss prevailed upon her son to adopt a pseudonym for the occasion. His ironic choice was "Andrew Lee," borrowed from one of Priscilla's ancestors, a clergyman who allegedly had cursed any of his descendants who might smoke or take a drink; in *A Writer's Capital* Auchincloss muses upon the good parson's possible reaction to seeing his own name affixed to a work of fiction dealing with the frivolities of the idle rich. In any case, somewhat to the surprise of both mother and son, the novel was rather well received; thereafter, Auchincloss would publish his writing under his own name, applied also to subsequent editions of *The Indifferent Children*.

Taking its title from the same scene in *Hamlet* that would later inspire both the title and the action of Tom Stoppard's 1967 play *Rosencrantz and Guildenstern Are Dead*, *The Indifferent Children* focuses upon what Thorstein Veblen more than a generation earlier had stigmatized as the "leisure class," those with more money, and hence more spare time, than they know what to do with. The principal character, stigmatized in advance with the name of Beverly Stregelinus, is a totally "useless" young man, a social drone and ideal "extra man" at parties until World War II intrudes upon his carefully disorganized existence. Both Rosencrantz and Guildenstern combined, Beverly, too, must die, if only as a means of removing him from the scene and bringing the novel to an end.

As Auchincloss relates in *A Writer's Capital,* the character of Beverly Stregelinus was the product of a long and somewhat complex evolution, originating in the author's curious friendship with the late Jack Woods. Woods, the writer's close friend and sometime Yale roommate, was by his origins a true "outsider," a youth of modest origins with few resources save for his brains and talent, his strong ambition flawed by deep-seated emotional problems; at the time of his death by suicide in 1941, Woods was, according to Auchincloss, considered as a rising young journalist on the threshold of a brilliant career. In any case, Woods, during the brief span of his friendship with Auchincloss, appears to have functioned as both midwife and goad to his friend's literary talent and ambitions; the name of Beverly Stregelinus was in fact invented by Woods himself, to designate a sort of Auchincloss caricature, the type of character, indeed, that Priscilla Auchincloss seems to have feared that her second son might become. The personage of Beverly, as developed by Auchincloss in concert and conversation with Jack Woods, was in fact to have been the protagonist of the planned second novelistic effort, begun in 1938; by the time a third novel began to emerge at war's end, after Woods's death, the war itself had intervened, providing a most ironic backdrop for the actions of such a character as the one that he and Woods had developed.

Although the autobiographical elements in the character of Beverly are at times readily apparent, Auchincloss wisely chose to present Beverly as a character substantially older than himself; born in 1910, Beverly has experienced the 1920s as an adolescent, completing preparatory school and entering Yale before the onset of the Great Depression. He is also of an age to have been in the forefront of the "café society" of the middle to late 1930s, a bizarre social phenomenon that he to a great extent personifies.

The action of *The Indifferent Children,* augmented by frequent flashbacks, begins in the summer of 1941 when Beverly at last loses the job, or the excuse for one, that has sustained him for most of the previous decade. Like his creator, Beverly is a Yale alumnus who has attended law school at the University of Virginia; unlike Auchincloss, however, Beverly found little interest in the law and cut short his studies after the first year, harboring vague aspirations to be a poet or playwright. Since that time, for want of something better to do, he had been nominally employed by the long-suffering Felix Salberg as a sales representative in the latter's art gallery. His main occupation, however, is party-going, supplemented by lunches and other gossip sessions, often over the telephone, with middle-aged society matrons. On a June day in 1941 it all catches up with him when Felix once again upbraids him for his chronic tardiness and finally accepts Beverly's oft-tended, pro forma resignation, much to Beverly's surprise. At age thirty-one, Beverly is without a job and, as he has long since inwardly suspected, without any real shape or definition to his life.

The obvious question, frequently posed throughout the novel, is whether or not America's imminent involvement in World War II will help Beverly Stregelinus to find or define himself, as it did for some men but not for others. Auchincloss himself appears to have left the question unanswered in his mind for quite some time; in a wry preface appended to later paperback editions of the book, he observes, "As

Beverly Stregelinus would come to see his own absurdity in the absurdity of his fellow bureaucrats, he would be redeemed and emerge as a serious person. But he simply refused ever quite to do as he was told, and in the end I threw a bomb at him." In any case, the character of Beverly as revealed and, in a sense, developed, allows for little true growth. Like Rosencrantz and Guildenstern, Stregelinus is essentially a parasite, dependent upon a generous host for sustained nourishment; he is therefore unfit for survival in the changed postwar world; indeed, given his own postwar perspective, Auchincloss had little other choice than to end Beverly's life in 1944; still in uniform, Beverly is disintegrated by a buzz bomb as he prepares to join an incongruous gathering of middle-aged, noble ladies in war-ravaged London.

Throughout the narrative, Auchincloss retains just enough compassion for his heavily satirized protagonist that his redemption seems barely possible, if not likely. Beverly is sufficiently intelligent, and basically decent, to perceive the yawning gaps in his life, even as he allows his protracted adolescence to drag on into his thirties. His one romantic attachment, to the daughter of one of his socialite friends, is remarkable for its generosity: Sylvia Tremaine, born to Mrs. Arleus Stroud during her first marriage, has been left permanently lamed by the epidemic that killed her father in 1918. Sylvia's mother Angeline, perhaps half in love with Beverly herself, secretly hopes that he will eventually marry Sylvia, nicknamed "Syvvie." Notwithstanding, the relationship, such as it is, has lasted at least as long as Beverly's problematic employment at the Salberg gallery, with no immediate resolution in sight. The war then intervenes, coinciding roughly with Beverly's unemployment and a sharp decline in the investment income of his widowed mother, Amy Means Stregelinus, for whose father, a bishop, young Beverly was named.

Not long after losing his job, Beverly dutifully applies for a commission in the navy; initially rejected for want of useful skills, he eventually obtains an advanced commission (as lieutenant junior grade) through the strength of his acquaintances, a process which he decently, if arrogantly, denigrates as "pull." Like Auchincloss himself, Beverly finds his first billet in Naval Intelligence and is sent to Panama where, again moving parallel to his creator, he is assigned to the basically redundant Office of Naval Information. Sidelined from the war itself, set to the performance of numerous useless tasks, the officers in the Canal Zone have quickly built up more than their share of resentments and petty rivalries. Beverly, although disinclined by nature to take part in such backbiting, soon finds himself more deeply involved than he would care to be, thanks mainly to his growing involvement with the treacherous, overeducated Audrey Emerson who works in his office as a secretary.

Borrowed and developed from Auchincloss's first unpublished novel, Audrey Emerson is in many ways a prototype of the author's later female protagonists, well-read and strong-willed. Unlike her successors, however, Audrey harbors a strong if unconscious tendency toward malice. Whenever she is bored, which is often, she becomes meddlesome with little regard for the possible consequences. Beverly, whose tendency toward gossip is basically benign, fails fatally to perceive beneath Audrey's gossipy ways the heart and soul of a blackmailer. Audrey, of course, is herself too well bred to indulge in actual blackmail, but she is quick to use Beverly's incautious chatter to her own perceived advantage, however transitory that may be. Physically and emotionally attracted to Beverly, jealous of his preexisting relationship with Sylvia Tremaine, Audrey is nonetheless painfully aware of Beverly's frivolity and superfluity; no doubt she secretly hates herself for falling prey to his lounge-lizard charms. Feeling spurned by Beverly, Audrey happily betrays him to his commanding officer, Sheridan Gilder, a character quite as treacherous and spiteful as she. Her betrayal leads, in turn, to what must be seen as the novel's principal incident, an incongruous court-martial procedure in which Beverly, thanks to his year of law school, finds himself acting as defense counsel to the officer whom he had denounced in Audrey's presence.

Notable for its simultaneously realistic and satirical portrayal of military character and procedure, the protracted court-martial scene serves also as the climax of the novel; the trial will in fact backfire upon its perpetrators, Audrey and Gilder, leaving the latter permanently discredited and the former out of a job. Beverly, although somewhat tarred by the same brush, has far less at stake since he has no intention of remaining in the postwar navy. Unfortunately, he again succumbs to Audrey's dubious charms, causing the resentful, jealous Gilder to mention their relationship in an unsigned poison-pen letter to Sylvia Tremaine, to whom Beverly is still officially engaged. Gilder, of course, has no reason to suspect Sylvia's incipient instability and is secretly appalled to learn of her subsequent suicide. Beverly, for reasons deliberately left ambiguous, decides to honor Sylvia's memory by refusing to continue or pursue his relationship with Audrey, whose meddlesome nature has all but escaped his notice. The long novel ends rather abruptly, following a synopsis of Beverly's subsequent naval career; transferred to the amphibious service, Beverly takes an anonymous part in the Normandy landings and is killed not long thereafter when a misfired buzz bomb lands in Trafalgar Square. The scene of Beverly's death, likened by the unnamed narrator within the novel to the fall of the bridge of San Luis Rey in Thornton Wilder's novel of the same name, is somehow even less plausible than Sylvia Tremaine's suicide; it is thus quite likely that the author, as he later claimed, had grown tired of his main character and was hard pressed to finish him off.

Longer than any of Auchincloss's subsequent novels, including *The Rector of Justin,* although considerably shorter than the average novel of Marquand or O'Hara, *The Indifferent Children* might well have profited from judicious cutting. By reason of its length, moreover, the narrative implies a greater interest in the character of Beverly Stregelinus than can truly be justified on the part of either author or reader. Over the years since, one of the most recurrent criticisms of Auchincloss's novels has been that his characters are simply boring, of more interest to themselves than to the potential reader. While such an argument is often open to refutation, it seems unfortunately true in the case of Beverly Stregelinus and even that of Sylvia Tremaine; the average reader might well find it difficult to mourn them when they die, perhaps not even caring whether or not they ever lived. Audrey Emerson, for all her treacherous complexity, is quite another matter, capable of sustaining the reader's interest, if not sympathy, despite her relatively minor part in the action. Although *The Indifferent Children* received generally favorable reviews, it is perhaps no accident that Auchincloss chose to focus his two subsequent novels on the thoughts and actions of strong female characters.

Sybil and *A Law for the Lion*:

Back at the firm of Sullivan and Cromwell after completing *The Indifferent Children,* Auchincloss also worked hard at his writing, initially producing the short stories published in book form during 1950 as *The Injustice Collectors.* His second novel, *Sybil,* did not appear until 1951, shortly before his decision to devote full-time to his writing. *A Law for the Lion,* the principal product of his two-year furlough from the practice of law, was published in 1953. Both novels deal in depth with the patterns and problems of marriage in the postwar period, shown mainly from the viewpoint of the wife: *A Law for the Lion*, in particular, was identified by many reviewers as a powerful polemic in favor of legal reforms with regard to divorce, particularly in the state of New York. Auchincloss, although still unmarried by his middle thirties, showed unusual skill in his analyses of modern marriage, and particularly of the ways in which that institution had been affected by the recent upheavals and dislocations of World War II.

Sybil Rodman, the principal and title character of Auchincloss's second published novel, is, like Audrey Emerson, a bookish, introspective type, especially knowledgeable in the field of European history. Unlike Audrey, however, she is little inclined toward malice or intrigue, instinctively preferring the peace and quiet of her own company. Her marriage in 1941 to Philip Hilliard, a law-school classmate of her brother's, takes her somewhat by surprise, so resigned is she to serving as social secretary to the rich aunt upon whom her own family depends for support. Once committed, however, Sybil gives freely of herself, quite in contrast to the objective, methodical Philip for whom marriage is, first and foremost, a social and professional necessity. Brought together, no doubt, by the proverbial attraction of opposites, hastened into marriage by the threat of American involvement in the war, the Hilliards are in fact quite ill matched, estranged even further by the inevitable separation that the war will bring. Philip, true to his nature, has few inhibitions about adultery, especially during wartime; Sybil, meanwhile, remains faithful to Philip and, quite inadvertently, manages to ingratiate herself with her husband's previously hostile relatives. Upon returning from the navy to his Manhattan law practice, Philip grows increasingly restive under the benign grasp of Sybil's unquestioning devotion and in time seeks out the rather more boisterous companionship of Julia Anderton, whom he was "seeing" when he first met Sybil and who, inexplicably to some if not to others, has never married.

Julia Anderton, to be sure, recalls the darker side of Audrey Emerson, even as she lacks the intellectual dimension that Audrey shares with Sybil. Tall, blonde, and blunt of manner, undeniably attractive, Julia in her late twenties wryly reflects that gentlemen apparently prefer bookish, retiring types like Sybil Rodman, at least when choosing wives. Perhaps less observant than Audrey, although equally calculating, Julia is more than ripe for an affair, nor has she ever really dropped the torch that she once carried for Philip. Philip, in his characteristic methodical way, decides that the time has come for an infatuation and proceeds to fall deliberately and completely in love with his "old flame," who in turn is quick to press her advantage toward becoming the second Mrs. Philip Hilliard.

At first resigned to her apparent fate, Sybil Rodman Hilliard in time finds the inner resources to deny her husband his requested divorce, arguing in part that she is attempting to "rescue" him from the predatory Julia. Behind her decision also is her dissatisfaction with divorce laws as they currently exist, and as they have been explained to her by Nicholas Cummings, her attorney and also her first cousin: To obtain a divorce in New York, she would have to prove Philip's adultery in court, and in order to apply elsewhere, perhaps in Nevada, she would in effect have to commit perjury, falsely stating her intentions to establish permanent residence. Philip, weak and indecisive beneath the surface, finds himself outmaneuvered not only by his wife and mistress but also by his mother, Sybil's defender and advocate. Not altogether unwillingly, he renounces Julia and returns to Sybil, only to be caught unprepared when Sybil abruptly leaves him, having at last perceived the lack of a true common bond between them.

After defying her husband on the question of divorce and remarriage, Sybil subsequently develops the courage of her own convictions, moving from passivity to deliberate action. Upon leaving Philip, however, she quickly learns that she has overstepped the invisible boundaries laid down by earlier generations, particularly her parents' generation. To the older folk, accustomed to silent suffering, Sybil's rejection of her returned husband constitutes an intolerable act of rebellion, surely a product of the new, permissive postwar morality. Thus ostracized by her former protectors, Sybil proceeds in search of herself, in time embarking on an affair of her own with Howard Plimpton, whom she had befriended long before her marriage to Philip. Howard, a former stockbroker who has abandoned wife and job to try his hand at landscape painting, is perhaps even more demonstrably a renegade than Sybil herself. Significantly, it is Sybil who seeks to reinstate their former friendship; Howard, truly in flight from his former life, would just as soon be left alone in his attic studio. Also significantly, it is not Philip Hilliard himself but his mother, Lucy, Sybil's former defender, who hires private detectives to spy on Sybil and Howard when there is in fact little or nothing to report; only after learning of the surveillance does Sybil press the reticent Howard to consummate their affair, if only to live up to the bad name her mother-in-law has given her. Philip, dense and uncomprehending as ever, wallows in self-pity over the way

the women in his life have treated him. In time the Hilliards will again
be "reconciled," at least in a manner of speaking: They will resume life
as a couple, as the line of least resistance against the strong pressure
exerted by both families.

Remarkable for its portrayal of the complex, developing title character, *Sybil* offers also a credible and entertaining portrayal of New York
society in the immediate prewar and postwar years, a period when the
so-called generation gap yawned for what may well have been the first
time. Sybil Rodman, born in 1919, shares little with the previous
generation, much as she might honestly prefer to share the values in-
culcated by her parents and their friends. Against her nature and at
times against her will, Sybil finds that her integrity has made of her a
rebel, and that her personal approach to "common sense" is all too
frequently mistaken for pure self-indulgence. As Auchincloss himself
has observed of Marquand's *Point of No Return,* the American novel of
manners in the mid-twentieth century often veers off toward the psychological, and *Sybil* is a case in point. While the elder Rodmans and
Hilliards belong to the novel of manners, Sybil herself does not—at
least not until the end of the novel, when she makes the long-awaited
"accommodation" to her situation and to society. As a character, she is
of interest mainly for her psychological makeup and development, precisely those qualities most likely to be varnished over by society. Philip
Hilliard, meanwhile, remains almost too close to stereotype to elicit
the reader's full belief, serving mainly as a convenient foil to his wife's
transformation.

A *Law for the Lion*

Auchincloss's subsequent novel, *A Law for the Lion,* may be seen in
many respects as a revised, expanded, and somewhat deepened revision
of *Sybil,* featuring a similar set of characters who make their situation
rather more complex than the one represented in the earlier novel.
George Dilworth, like Philip Hilliard, is a Wall Street lawyer; unlike
Philip, however, he is clearly and carefully differentiated: The son of a
New Hampshire parson, George has succeeded on Wall Street through
careful, dedicated practice of the values that he *thinks* he learned as a
child, espousing the law with a devotion denied to either of his wives.
Losing his first wife to tuberculosis soon after his elevation to partnership in the firm of Hunt and Livermore, Dilworth then turns his dis-
tracted attentions toward the acquisition of a second spouse, primarily

as a stepmother for his school-age daughter Hilda, named for her mother.

The most likely candidate turns out to be one Eloise, the niece and de facto ward of George's senior partner, Gerald Hunt. Eloise, the daughter of Hunt's much-married expatriate sister by the long-forgotten first husband killed in World War I, was a recent graduate of Barnard College at the time; her plans to join her mother, Irene, in Europe had just been foiled by Irene's remarriage to a man named Bleecker and their subsequent removal to India. At the very least, the prospect of marriage to George Dilworth strikes Eloise as more promising than that of continued dependence upon her Uncle Gerald and Aunt Gladys; soon after the marriage, Eloise proceeds to bear George two daughters of their own.

The action of the novel begins some thirteen years after Eloise's marriage to George, when Irene Bleecker comes to New York for emergency surgery, then appears to have returned to the United States for good. George, never tolerant of his mother-in-law's personality, lifestyle, or behavior, soon finds her presence intolerable and orders her out of his house, claiming that her bohemian manners and occasional heavy drinking threaten to corrupt his and Eloise's young daughters. Although Eloise outwardly submits to George's will, the incident widens many latent gaps in the Dilworths' marriage by revealing to Eloise the basic disparity between their two natures. More like her mother than she has ever cared to admit, at least in an atmosphere controlled by George and by her uncle Gerald, Eloise seeks out the companionship of some bohemian friends from her Barnard years and soon befriends a disaffected young writer named Carl Landik, well known for a recent novel derived from his service with the U.S. Marines during World War II. Careful to define their relationship as a platonic one, Eloise accompanies Landik to plays, concerts, and the like; George, generally too busy for such things, accords his tacit permission until alerted by two meddlers of the dangers implicit in the situation. One of the meddlers is Irene, whose intention is to remind George that he has been neglecting her daughter, who remains attractive to other men; the other meddler is George's longtime friend and partner Harry Hamilton, whose motivations are somewhat more complex.

Harry, a confirmed bachelor intensely devoted to the memory of George's first wife Hilda, has always resented Eloise's usurpation of Hilda's place and welcomes the opportunity to discredit Eloise in George's eyes. Once alerted, George meets the threat with the same uncompromising stance that he has used on Irene, categorically forbidding Eloise to see any more of Landik. Eloise, meanwhile, has stopped listening to George after yielding to him in the matter of her mother; she meets his prohibition with open defiance, proceeding thereafter to instigate an affair with Landik as an expression of her outrage. Unfortunately for all, the calculating Harry Hamilton has foreseen everything, even arranging for the presence of detectives and photographers at the time and place of the couple's initial assignation. Thus armed with proof of adultery, required grounds for divorce in the state of New York, Harry then urges an outraged George to file both for divorce and for full custody of the minor children, magnanimously offering to handle the case himself. George, ignoring Gerald Hunt's warnings that the publicity attending divorce proceedings against Hunt's own niece might do irreparable damage to the firm, refuses to consider alternatives or modify his demands, even at the eventual cost of his own resignation—and Harry's. Once his wishes have been granted, George, in an ironic final gesture, offers to give Eloise all that she has been denied in court—custody, alimony, child support, even the possibility of reconciliation—and is quite unprepared for her refusal to accept anything but custody of the children. Eloise has had her taste of freedom and found it exhilarating; refusing George, refusing even Landik, she has embarked at last upon a career of her own—in publishing—with an enthusiasm that George, at forty-seven some thirteen years her senior, is quite unable to understand.

Like Sybil Hilliard and Audrey Emerson in Auchincloss's earlier novels, Eloise Dilworth is intelligent, perceptive, and well-read, with a pronounced intellectual bent. Unlike her predecessors, she has had the questionable example of an unorthodox, iconoclastic mother, who from the start has suggested the presence of a "world" quite different from that represented by George and his mentor Gerald Hunt. Although less a mother to Eloise than a kind of wayward, exotic elder sister, Irene—known by her first name even to her granddaughters—provides a useful, even wise corrective to her brother's hidebound traditionalism and her son-in-law's dehumanizing devotion to his work. Indeed, it is from Irene's outspoken manner that Eloise will derive the perspectives—and much of the strength—necessary to her implied survival. Irene, meanwhile, emerges from the narrative as one of the author's more entertaining, even engaging minor characters, enjoying a final victory of her own through yet another marriage—to the rich banker Arthur Irwin, an old friend whose support of Eloise's cause has helped to force George Dilworth's resignation from the firm of Hunt and Livermore.

Although far from "liberated" when viewed or judged from the perspectives, or by the standards, of a later generation, both Irene Bleecker and her daughter bear witness to the emergence of a feminine consciousness which, even during the immediate postwar years, posed an increasing challenge to the traditional assumptions of the male-dominated establishment. "One law for the lion and ox is oppression," wrote William Blake in the passage that Auchincloss chose for both his title and his epigraph; men, he implied, would soon be obliged to reconsider having written the lion's share of the law in their own favor, at least in matters of divorce and possibly in other areas as well.

Despite the superficial similarities, *A Law for the Lion* becomes, in the final analysis, a stronger and more satisfying accomplishment than *Sybil,* owing mainly to the author's increasing skill in the delineation and development of character. Whereas Sybil Rodman develops against a generally stereotypical background of major and minor characters, Eloise Dilworth will discover herself in conflict with worthy, colorful adversaries, in particular the complex, complacent Harry Hamilton. Quite probably a repressed homosexual, in any case a remarkable instance of arrested emotional development, the mountainous, overbearing Harry would emerge as a humorous character were it not for his potential danger, to himself as well as to others. For Harry, even more than for George, the law serves as a last refuge of order in a threateningly disordered world; to its practitioners, moreover, it provides rare and awesome power. Long resentful of Eloise, who somehow failed to welcome him as a "third party" to her marriage the way Hilda Dilworth did, Harry Hamilton plunges into the divorce proceeding with near-manic zeal and fervor, transcending the limits of George's own righteous indignation. Uncannily, he manages to predict and manipulate Eloise's actions, first with Landik and later in the courtroom. It is Harry, moreover, whose intransigence hastens his and George's departure from the firm where both men have worked for twenty years.

Even more than *Sybil, A Law for the Lion* reaches beyond the novel of manners toward the novel of psychological analysis, showing increased concern with the motivation of characters. Although, as noted above, many reviewers found it a powerful polemic against the divorce laws of the time, its ultimate interest moves well beyond the documentary level, offering a full cast of complex characters who resist reduction to stereotype. Throughout the action, moreover, Auchincloss interweaves Eloise's story with that of the younger Hilda Dilworth, George's daughter by his first marriage, presumably in an effort to expand the novel's scope. Hilda, at the time of the story, is at the same age and stage of life as Eloise when she married George; a recent graduate of Vassar, she works as a secretary in what George rather condescendingly calls an "uptown" Manhattan law firm. Attracted to the colorful, slightly raffish junior partner, Bobbie Chapin, Hilda works out her personal destiny in counterpoise to that of her stepmother, in whom she alternately sees a positive and negative example: In one of the novel's rather less plausible twists, Bobbie Chapin steps forward to represent Eloise in the divorce proceedings. At the end of the novel the author centers his attention upon Bobbie and Hilda as they work out their differences, leaving the implication that they may succeed where George and Eloise have failed.

The Shift to Wall Street Novels

During the last half of the 1950s Auchincloss strengthened and deepened his reputation with three perceptive studies of the postwar professional man, more or less following the lead established by Marquand in *Point of No Return* (1949). The Wall Street milieu, which served as little more than background for the stories of Sybil Hilliard and Eloise Dilworth, becomes the primary focus of the author's attention in his three subsequent novels as it shifts from the wife to the husband in each couple. As before, the analysis of modern marriage looms large in the author's exposition, but in the three novels of the late 1950s marriage is shown as only one of several relationships that contrive to shape or test a man's character; of equal or greater importance, suggests Auchincloss, is the man's relationship to his chosen profession. In *A Law for the Lion* George Dilworth is shown as a man who has chosen to define himself through his trade, neglecting his family in the process; George, however, remains a minor character, overshadowed by his late-blooming second wife. He is known to practice law, but is never actually shown doing so; in the three subsequent novels Auchincloss will examine the working life of lawyers and bankers in exhaustive, meticulous detail, showing how human lives can be permanently altered by the smallest change in "fine print," or in the reading thereof. As before, however, his emphasis is not upon documentation but rather upon character, showing the interactions of person and profession within the working of a single human mind.

The Great World and Timothy Colt; Venus In Sparta

Developed from a short story of the same name initially published
in *The Romantic Egoists* (1954), *The Great World and Timothy Colt* is
perhaps the strongest and most memorable of Auchincloss's early novels, notable for its portrayal of a true "outsider's" ascent toward the
upper reaches of privilege and power. Timothy Colt, unlike the lawyers
portrayed in Auchincloss's earlier novels, is a product of the New York
City public school system who has worked his way through college and
law school at Columbia University. The only offspring of an odd marriage between an aging New York bachelor and his Ohio-born nurse,
Timothy matured early, assuming the burdens of his increasingly alcoholic widowed mother in addition to his own. Indeed, the only bond
that Colt shares with Auchincloss's earlier fictional lawyers is that of
birth and residence in New York City. His wife, Ann, is no more
privileged by background than he, having grown up as the only daughter of a New Jersey real-estate broker. Both Colts, however, are well
educated and intelligent, believing implicitly in the principle of meritocracy. True to these beliefs, Timmy Colt rises rapidly in the Wall
Street law firm of Sheffield, Knox, and Dale under the tutelage of
Henry Knox, like George Dilworth a minister's son from New England
who has succeeded in New York legal practice without feeling the need
to sacrifice his ideals. In a sense, Knox is as much an outsider as Timmy
Colt himself, and it is their shared idealism that draws the two men
together.

Knox, unlike Timmy Colt, is a scholar and philosopher of the law;
having failed to arouse similar gifts in Timmy, he soon observes that
his young protege is in fact an "artist" of the law, with an instinctive
sense of fitness and proportion. Quite probably, Knox reflects, Timmy's gifts are even rarer and more valuable than his own, at least in
their common field of corporate law. Rising rapidly toward partnership, Timmy, unwilling to delegate authority, is soon doing most of
the firm's corporate work; it is not long before his extreme devotion to
duty begins to undermine his family life and to threaten his health as
well. Significantly, Timmy's dedication derives not from ambition—
he shows little interest in the prospect of partnership—but rather from
the same determination, underlain by simple stubbornness, that thus
far has assured his escape from the shabby hotel-room milieu in which
his mother reared him. In short, his rise is fueled less by the desire for
success than by his fear of failure.

Like his mentor Henry Knox, albeit for somewhat different reasons, Timothy Colt cherishes an ideal of the law, in Timmy's case a Pythagorean unity in which all pieces might be made to fit. Absorbed in the solution of the problems set before him, Timmy finds that he has little time left for social life; in the meantime, his self-absorption has become so nearly total that he has failed to perceive the unavoidable realities of "office politics": Unknown to him, he has become identified as Knox's favorite among the associates, credited also with his mentor's rather prudish arrogance.

The firm of Sheffield, Knox, and Dale, it seems, has been reassembled from loose parts by none other than Henry Knox himself upon the demise of the former senior partners. Sheffield, a mere nonentity in the original firm, has been elevated by Knox to elder-statesman status; well past eighty at the time of the novel's action, he rarely practices law at all, though he has yet to retire. Sheridan Dale, at fifty-seven a year younger than Knox, is not only an outsider but an intruder, a Fordham Law graduate whose presence in the firm Knox tolerates merely because it preceded his own: In the complex scheme of New York professional society it might be inferred that Dale, the product of a Jesuit education, is of Roman Catholic and possibly Irish origins, although such facts are not explicitly stated in the novel. Upon joining the firm as a clerk, with Dale already in place, Knox attempted to befriend Dale until Dale showed a tendency toward sharp practice, bordering upon and at times exceeding dishonesty. Dale further offended Knox by suggesting that all lawyers are alike, attempting to "shave" the law in favor of their clients. Knox, refusing any possible common bond with Dale, has treated him thereafter with little more than marginal civility, regardless of Dale's marriage around the age of forty to a widowed socialite and his subsequent cultivation of the rich and influential, potential clients of his Estate Division; Dale, meanwhile, has come to dismiss Knox as a Harvard-educated snob. Timmy Colt, predictably, shares his mentor's view of Dale. It is thus a deliberate affront of both men when Dale requests Timmy Colt's services on a corporate transaction involving one George Emlen, the nephew of Dale's wife Clarissa.

Blunt of manner and rather uncouth, unmarried and still living with his mother, George Emlen soon emerges as Timmy Colt's personal nemesis, quick to spot and exploit the feelings of inadequacy that underlie Timmy's exceptional drive. Timmy, conscientious as usual, can never seem quite to satisfy George, or to avoid the latter's insults. The transaction, involving George's purchase of several textile mills, lasts through the summer and into the fall; to celebrate its conclusion, George throws a party at which he makes fun of Timmy as usual. Timmy, near the breaking point from overwork, publicly returns the insult, a breach of etiquette for which he is expected to apologize. At first disinclined to do so, even on the advice of Henry Knox, Timmy finally yields to the entreaties of his wife Ann, warning her that she alone will be responsible for whatever happens to them afterward. In Timmy's mind at least, the apology marks a distinct turning point in his career and in their lives, the moment at which he "sells out" his ideals to the "great world" personified by Sheridan Dale and George Emlen.

Once he has apologized to George, Timmy Colt goes even further, announcing to an astonished Knox his intention to work thereafter for Sheridan Dale. Henry Knox, known to be in precarious health, expires several hours later of a heart attack, leaving Timmy with the guilty secret of their rupture. For Timmy, however, the die has been cast, and the "sellout" will become complete: As a partner in the new firm organized by Dale after Knox's death, Timmy Colt in effect becomes Dale's "hatchet man," charged with streamlining office procedure; acting with his usual skill and concentration, he manages to alienate nearly everyone in the office. He has chosen his path, however, and there is no turning back.

True to form, Timmy never fails to remind Ann of her shared responsibility for the course that their lives have taken. Ann, increasingly horrified at the changes in Timmy's manner and behavior, fails to see the connection and in time they separate, unable to reconcile their differences yet unwilling to proceed with a divorce. It is at the start of the separation that Timmy meets Sheridan Dale's stepdaughter, Eileen Shallcross, recently divorced from a Maryland sportsman. Sophisticated, yet oddly vulnerable to Timmy's marginal charms, Eileen at first assumes the role of Timmy's confidante and cultural guide, escorting him to museums, plays, and concerts; his rapid rise has hitherto left little time for such distractions. Well aware of their mutual attraction, Timmy and Eileen nonetheless defer the consummation of their love for several months, initially preferring the rare benefits of friendship. Timmy, meanwhile, finds his legal practice increasingly concerned with the financial affairs of Eileen's mother, Clarissa Dale, and their various relatives, including George Emlen and his mother, Florence.

Despite the apology and his increasing involvement with the extended Dale clan, Timmy detests George Emlen quite as heartily as before, having learned not to trust him. With the approaching maturity of an Emlen family trust, Timmy, named by Dale as a trustee, suspects George of plotting to steal, in effect, from his younger sisters, and it is not long before he seeks and finds the evidence he needs: George, it seems, has offered his sisters a cash settlement in exchange for stock in an apparently worthless textile mill; his sisters, meanwhile, do not mind at all; they have both married grasping, improvident men and have a seemingly constant need for ready cash. Timmy, conscientious as usual, confronts both Dale and his nephew with the evidence of valuable patents involved in the transaction, patents that will leave George Emlen far richer than his sisters. Dale, of course, has been privy to the scheme all along, and might even have devised it himself. In time, abandoning his last scruples, Timmy will join the conspiracy by remaining silent; even so, he experiences remorse and confesses his collusion to Eileen, who in a rare moment of indiscretion confides the secret to her cousin Anita Ferguson, the elder of George Emlen's two sisters. By that time, the division of property has already been made, owing mainly to Anita's pressing need for money; redressment, if any, must be made through the courts.

When his turn comes to testify, Timmy Colt behaves oddly in character by confessing to the cover-up, assuming full responsibility so as not to implicate either Sheridan Dale or George Emlen. In a sense the confession is gratuitous, since no charges could ever have been proved against him; in another sense, it is a gesture of self-serving heroics that can only discredit the firm even as it bids fair to ruin Timmy's own career. Timmy, however, is past caring, having at last come to terms with his own conscience at the cost of resigning from the firm. Reconciled with Ann for the second time, Timmy faces an uncertain future but will probably not be disbarred.

Strengthened by Auchincloss's authentic rendering of the Wall Street business atmosphere, *The Great World and Timothy Colt* compares favorably with the best work of O'Hara and Marquand, even transcending that work through Auchincloss's approach to character. Caught between the real and the ideal, Timmy Colt is truly a romantic egoist, a hero turned loose amid the mundane. Curiously, Timmy is said to have derived little satisfaction from his wartime service as a naval officer, let alone an occasion for heroism; to his way of thinking the war was a bore, a four-year interruption in the ongoing practice of law. His decision, before and after Knox's death, to join the "great world" of sharp practice is truly that of the disillusioned romantic, the Faust who sells his soul. At bottom, however, the transaction is never complete; even as Dale's confederate, he retains his sense of values but still he declines to act upon it. Although strongly attracted to Eileen Shallcross and all that she appears to represent, he turns his back upon her after learning of her "treachery," quite unmoved when she subsequently testifies in his behalf. Like Nick Carraway in Fitzgerald's *The Great Gatsby*, Timmy Colt has learned, or believes himself to have learned, that such "beautiful people" are accountable only among themselves, hence not to be trusted by others.

In his presentation of Timmy Colt, Auchincloss recovers much of the ironic detachment implicit in his portrayal of Beverly Stregelinus, yet oddly absent from his two intervening novels. Timmy Colt, for all his evident qualities, is seldom the author's true spokesman and more frequently his stooge, quixotic and inflexible. Eileen Shallcross, by contrast, is revealed as a more dimensional and sympathetic character than Timmy can ever appreciate; in any event, Timmy's absolute categories leave little room for Eileen's redeeming qualities, causing him to classify her unfairly among her less commendable relatives. Those same categories cause him to accept Ann without question, presumably since she has long since agreed to share his life; as a result, their marriage, although perhaps basically sound, will never really grow or develop. At the end of the novel, a number of questions that Timmy has answered to his own satisfaction thus remain unresolved for the reader, as no doubt for the author himself.

Although perhaps poorly equipped to face the future, Timmy Colt at least remains alive. For Michael Farish, the ill-starred "hero" of *Venus in Sparta*, exoneration on similar charges of sharp practice will fail to provide a reprieve. Like O'Hara's Julian English, Michael will find himself propelled toward suicide, perhaps inexorably, by a suddenly menacing series of small choices and random encounters. As much threatened by success as by failure, Michael has in fact left himself little choice.

Unlike Timmy Colt, Michael Farish has been born to privilege, but in Michael's case such privilege is not without its burdens. As the only grandson of the founder of the Hudson River Trust Company, Michael Farish has always viewed the prospect of becoming its president with both anticipation and foreboding. Although his appointment would be a logical choice, it is by no means an automatic one: Due to Michael's father's death at the early age of thirty-eight, management of the bank has passed out of the Farish family, and Michael, throughout his long career with the bank, has had to establish his fitness for the job; in fact, he has succeeded. He has failed, however, to develop the self-confidence that would lend meaning to his success; at forty-five he remains insecure, threatened by nagging, generally unfounded doubts concerning his fitness either as a banker or as a man.

For Michael Farish, the downhill slide begins with the review of one of the bank's long-standing trusts, an account for which Michael was himself responsible and which helped to launch him on his steady rise within the bank. A minor lapse in procedure suddenly comes back to haunt him, at least in his own mind, casting discredit upon all that has happened to him since. At almost the same moment he discovers, or allows himself to discover, that his wife Flora, five years his senior, has taken a lover among his younger subordinates at the bank. In re-action, he seeks to reactivate a wartime love affair with Alida Meredith, daughter of the bank's current president and by now the daughter-in-law of Ambrose Parr, the tycoon who has become the bank's principal owner. Somewhat to his surprise, Michael discovers in time that he will not be punished by the dark forces that he fears. Cleared of any suspicion of wrongdoing in the matter of the Winters trust, success-fully divorced from Flora and remarried to Alida, Michael waits in vain for the lightning bolt that will destroy him, foreshadowed by the dark memories that haunt his waking hours. In the end, he openly courts disaster by breaking with Alida and beginning an affair with his former stepdaughter, Flora's child by her first husband. Having at last burnt all of his bridges behind him, Michael swims purposefully out to sea, mourned mainly by his widowed mother.

Like O'Hara's *Appointment in Samarra, Venus in Sparta* demands to be viewed less as a novel of manners than as a psychological novel with a strong social background. Although Michael's tribulations derive in part from the demands of his social position, his response to those demands is purely idiosyncratic and personal, the product of his own undeveloped emotions. Deprived of his father's approval and moral support due to the latter's early death, compelled into an early marriage to an older woman in an effort to prove his own manhood, quite unsure of his demonstrable interpersonal skills as a trust officer, Michael in-habits a private hell very largely of his own making: Like Timmy Colt, he has failed to develop a truly "human" side; he remains an enigma to his closest associates at the bank and will ultimately reject even

Alida's unquestioning love, freely offered as a disinterested gift. In a sense he is also, like Timmy, a romantic egoist, for whom even the best in life will be a disappointment.

Pursuit of the Prodigal

Reese Parmelee, the title character of Auchincloss's third "professional" or Wall Street novel, shares with Michael Farish the advantage of privileged birth and with Timmy Colt a dedication to the practice of law. Unlike either of his fictional predecessors, however, Reese Parmelee has been born with the soul of a rebel, grown restive under the implied constraints of a system in which he believes he is expected to function like one of the cogs in a well-oiled machine. *Pursuit of the Prodigal* thus veers back toward the novel of manners while offering a fully developed, generally plausible psychological portrait of its protagonist.

Like Charles Gray in Marquand's *Point of No Return,* unlike such earlier Auchincloss characters as Timmy Colt and George Dilworth, Reese Parmelee is possessed of a restless intelligence combined with a strong critical sense. Although he has attended all the "right" schools and has gone to work in his grandfather's old law firm, Reese has never felt that such choices were exactly right for him; he has never doubted the possibility that sooner or later even better options might present themselves. Following his return from World War II, Reese has gradually defined himself as a renegade, at times with romantic defiance, carefully distancing himself from "his world" as he prepares for an eventual escape. Taking as his mistress a former childhood friend, he willfully equates Cynthia's suburban boredom with his own deep-seated rebellion, only to leave her in disgust when she refuses to join him in self-imposed "exile." His wife Esther has disappointed him also, having come to love the entrenched family life for which she once shared his own thinly veiled contempt.

Severing his connection with the family law firm, Reese embarks on a cross-country trip to "clear his head." Returning to Manhattan, he rents a small flat in Greenwich Village, finding work not long thereafter in the uptown law firm of Amos Levine, whose courtroom performances are often featured in the news. Like Timmy Colt, Reese has entered the law with a strong sense of ethics, and despite an abiding personal fondness of Amos, he often suspects the latter of sharp practice. Amos, truly skillful at his trade, continues to parry Reese's suspicions, persuading him that he must be imagining things. Reese, meanwhile, has become increasingly involved in the life and career of Rosina Street, a Virginia-born magazine journalist who came to the Levine firm as a client and who will in time become Reese's second wife.

Throughout the novel, Auchincloss maintains active tension between Reese Parmelee's increasing willfulness and the strong pull of his background, a force exerted primarily by the behavior of both wives. Rosina Street, although she attracts Reese by reason of her different background and "working girl" life-style, soon cleaves to the life of Parmelee Cove, Long Island, as completely as did her predecessor, Esther Means. Esther, meanwhile, remains more entrenched in Parmelee Cove than ever, having married the prosperous brother of Reese's former mistress Cynthia; in time the two wives, and even Cynthia, will "join forces" against Reese, at least from Reese's point of view: At Esther's invitation, Reese, Rosina, and their daughter will become summer residents at Parmelee Cove. Alfred Parmelee, Reese's son by Esther, will follow his father to boarding school against the latter's objections, objections that helped to end Reese's marriage to Esther. Reese, now Amos Levine's full partner, continues to raise questions about Amos's tactics, never fully content with his partner's reassuring answers yet never fully able to discredit them. As Auchincloss observes in his preface to a 1965 softcover edition of the novel, "The 'establishment' of our day can no longer afford, like the father in the parable, to await the prodigal's return. It rushes after him, causing a stampede. It does not see him as a mutineer, but as a rat leaving a sinking ship." After running away once more, this time from Rosina, Reese will perceive both the petulance and the futility of his rebellion, returning both to her and to Amos's firm in a spirit of commitment mixed with resignation.

If Timmy Colt is Auchincloss's Don Quixote, Reese Parmelee is his Diogenes, applying to others the same standards of integrity that he demands of himself. Like Timmy, he is an idealist, a potentially ridiculous figure in the modern world, yet, unlike Timmy, he displays a reassuring humanity that leads him, in the end, toward rueful reconsideration of his own uncompromising positions. Even his idealism, about to be tempered by realism, stands as proof that, even were he to succeed in removing himself from Parmelee Cove, he could never remove Parmelee Cove from himself. It is Reese's particular relationship to his background, moreover, that marks *Pursuit of the Prodigal* as a return to the novel of manners.

Unlike Michael Farish of *Venus in Sparta,* Reese Parmelee is presented less as a psychological case history than as a more-or-less representative member of society, even as he perceives himself as a renegade imprisoned within that society against his will. Indeed, by his very individualism he exemplifies the desired product of the schools that he attended; if he is a "loner" by nature and preference, he is nevertheless the sort of man others perceive as a leader, and his efforts to escape will inevitably invite, against his wishes, the "pursuit" of emulation. Increasingly, however, the author's attention falls less upon Reese than upon his wives, and upon the friends, relatives, and acquaintances comprising his "society." The author's gift for satire, more evident here than in any of the novels since *The Indifferent Children,* provides a highly entertaining background with occasional flashes of humor. Of particular entertainment value are the renegade heiress Anstiss Stranahan and her husband Jack, who conduct a "salon" frequented by a motley assortment of artists, writers, editors, and hangers-on. Also of interest are Reese's parents, who lead a life of riding, skating, skiing, and tennis for want of anything better to do, yet are totally lacking in athletic talent. Esther Means Parmelee Coit, Reese's first wife, develops over the course of the novel into one of the author's more formidable creations, doubly formed by conflict with Reese and by her own sense of social fitness. Her second marriage, to the successful but insecure Phineas "Finny" Coit, is a coldly calculated act designed to assure not only her children's future but also Esther's position as the reigning "duchess" of Parmelee Cove.

With *Pursuit of the Prodigal,* Auchincloss completed his portrayal of the contemporary New York business and professional world. His subsequent novel, *The House of Five Talents,* would mark a significant departure in form, style, and approach, ushering in, with the new decade of the 1960s, the period of his greatest and most memorable accomplishments. Indeed, the time was no doubt at hand for him to attempt something new, if only for fear of repeating himself. For all of its merits *Pursuit of the Prodigal* is, at least on the surface, little different from the author's two previous novels, portraying again the tribulations of a lone male at odds with his working environment.

Auchincloss's portrayal of the "downtown" world, and of its effect upon those who work there, earned well-deserved praise among reviewers, many of whom saw his work as superior to that of Marquand or O'Hara; other reviewers, however, tended to see the New York background as too limiting and the typical Auchincloss character as unsympathetic, even boring. Michael Farish, in particular, struck some reviewers as implausible, others as simply uninteresting; in any case, Michael appeared unlikely to elicit the reader's interest in what would happen to him. To a greater or lesser degree, similar criticisms were also leveled against Timothy Colt and Reese Parmelee and would remain a familiar theme in journalistic criticism of subsequent Auchincloss novels, including such superior efforts as *The Embezzler.*

Chapter Four

The 1960s: Arrival and Establishment

Although Auchincloss by 1960 had earned for himself an enviable and even distinguished reputation in critical circles, he had yet to reach the wider audience upon whose attentions the strongest literary fortunes are built. With *The House of Five Talents,* published during that year, Auchincloss began to broaden the base of his readership, confirming his success throughout the decade with no fewer than three equally impressive novels: *Portrait in Brownstone* (1962), *The Rector of Justin* (1964), and *The Embezzler* (1966). During the same period he consolidated his reputation still further with the short fiction collected in *Powers of Attorney* (1963) and *Tales of Manhattan* (1967). His fifth and last novel of the decade, *A World of Profit* (1968), fell somewhat short of the mark established by its immediate predecessors, setting a trend toward repetition that would characterize many of his later novels. In retrospect, the entire decade of the 1960s must be seen as Auchincloss's strongest and most fruitful period, with increasing breadth of vision matched by maturing technical skills as a writer. Concerning the genesis of *The House of Five Talents,* Auchincloss wryly observes in *A Writer's Capital* that "the time came when irked by the insistence of critics and friends that the most important thing in the shaping of my characters had to be their money, I decided that it might be interesting to write the novel that everyone thought I had been writing." In order to do so, he continues, he had first to move his temporal focus backward in time: "I simply discovered that I could not write an interesting novel about the effect of an inherited fortune in the present day. The subject cried out for the last century, so I worked out my plot as the story of a great American fortune over a period of four generations." (*WC,* 124).

Ironically, the author's decision to move backward in time would eventually provide him with his richest material, yielding his greatest literary successes: Augusta Millinder, the narrator-protagonist of *The*

House of Five Talents, was born in 1873; Francis Prescott, the rector of *Justin,* as early as 1860. The major characters of *Portrait in Brownstone* and *The Embezzler* were all born, as were the author's own parents, during the decade of the 1880s. Arguably, the most credible and memorable of Auchincloss's characters are those who had reached or surpassed middle age by the 1930s, the decade of the author's own adolescence: That decade in particular, rendered with the authority of personal experience, acquires an added artistic dimension when projected through the ironic vision of older, wiser eyes.

For Auchincloss, the shift in time would also occasion, quite fortuitously, a striking shift in viewpoint as in narrative style. In each of his earlier novels he had favored a generally affectless third-person viewpoint, notable for its clarity and its often impersonal precision; his few ventures into first-person narration had thus far been confined to the shorter fictional forms. In *The House of Five Talents,* however, the fortyish male author would speak quite convincingly through the voice and selective recollections of a septuagenarian spinster; thereafter, in the three subsequent novels published prior to his fiftieth birthday, Auchincloss derives considerable artistic effect from the use of first-person narrative voices quite unlike his own, often combining multiple narratives and viewpoints within the same novel. The net result is that the characters quite literally appear to be speaking for themselves, from inside their own limitations, providing an immediacy of presentation that is all but impossible with third-person narration of the sort used in Auchincloss's earlier novels.

The House of Five Talents

Ostensibly written during 1948, in the shadow and aftermath of World War II, the fictional memoir that constitutes *The House of Five Talents* spans seven decades of rapid, irrevocable change in American society, tracing the effects upon the inheritors of a representative, if minor, American fortune of the late nineteenth century. The narrator, Miss Augusta Millinder, aged seventy-five and better known as "Gussie," functions within the narrative primarily as an observer, only occasionally as a participant. When she does participate, however, she records her involvement with a gusto to match her name, having at least heeded the advice of her sister-in-law: "If you must be an old maid, then be a magnificent old maid!"

Plainer than her sister Cora, who eventually marries a French noble-man, Gussie Millinder effectively chooses spinsterhood when she am-biguously breaks her engagement to Lancey Bell, a former suitor of Cora's who is well on his way toward a brilliant architectural career. As her narrative unfolds, Gussie will all but admit to an ingrained fear of men and marriage that undermines the supposed "principles" behind her crucial decision. In any case, she slowly develops into a keen ob-server, and occasional meddler, with regard to the morals and mar-riages of others; presaging many another of the celibate narrators to be found in Auchincloss's mature fiction, Gussie will come to take advan-tage of her unique position on the sidelines, the better to watch and record the action from an "objective" point of view.

By the time of Gussie's birth during 1873, the Millinder fortune, such as it is, is already well established and self-perpetuating, little dependent upon the halfhearted participation of Gussie's father and uncles. Her mother Eliza, as unimaginative as she is acquisitive, is by Gussie's own account the stronger if less admirable of her parents, ever competitive and especially alert to the presumably greater favors be-stowed by the Millinder fortune upon her brother-in-law Fred and his wife Daisy. It is Gussie who, shortly after the turn of the century, encourages her mother to collect art in a big way; it is also Gussie who attempts, in her first ill-fated effort at meddling, to disrupt her father's plans for divorce and subsequent remarriage to a stage actress. For much of her long life thereafter Gussie will act from conviction to intervene in the amatory and professional lives of her numerous and far-flung relatives, often with disastrous results. In one incident, pre-saging the plot of *The Embezzler,* Gussie agrees to rescue a cousin's husband from the threat of exposure and bankruptcy by "covering" the embezzled funds, yet only on condition that Collier Haven retire per-manently from business: A year of so later Gussie is so appalled by the effects of Haven's enforced idleness that she releases him from his vow. Predictably, perhaps, to all but Gussie, Collier Haven will return to his old ways, eventually fleeing the country as a fugitive from justice. In another incident, Gussie will force a marriage between her bohe-mian, fellow-traveling nephew Oswald and the showgirl whom he has impregnated; the marriage predictably fails, and within a few years Gussie has little choice but to adopt the child herself.

Among the novel's more engaging characters, besides Gussie Millin-der herself, is the widowed Ione Locke, a distant relation and accom-plished interior decorator, who in time becomes Gussie's sister-in-law.

At first the object of what seems a belated schoolgirl crush on Gussie's part, Ione, apart from the impoverished hangers-on who flock about Gussie in middle age, is perhaps her closest friend; notwithstanding, Ione's ardent, often flirtatious femininity continues to confound Gussie, who often mistakes it for disloyalty. Although the evidence is already at hand when Gussie first meets Ione, she can hardly believe that her new friend would want to marry her brother; sometime thereafter, Gussie successfully breaks Ione's liaison with a younger, unmarried male cousin, but only after her meddlesome attitude has "forced" the two would-be lovers to consummate their affair.

Set principally in New York City, with frequent excursions to the fashionable "watering places" of Newport and Bar Harbor, *The House of Five Talents* credibly evokes not only the so-called glories of the past but also the transitions of the novelistic present. In *A Writer's Capital* Auchincloss himself wonders if *The House of Five Talents,* "perhaps the most unusual book I have written," does not in fact belong more to history than to literature (*WC,* 124). To be sure, the plausible format of the fictional memoir all but dispenses with the need for plot, at least in the traditional sense, and Gussie Millinder's recollective musings at times assume a strong documentary flavor. Her aim, after all, has been to set the record straight, an aim set forth quite clearly in the novel's opening pages:

> Everyone wants to do something to the poor old past. The girls want to dramatize it. Alfred wants to dry-clean it. My nephew Oswald, who's been having such trouble recently with senate committees, wants to vilify it. Cora, who has forgotten her old resentments, wants to sentimentalize it. Leila Hoyt fills it with lovers, real and imagined, and her brother Lucius with his petty business triumphs. Perhaps Aunt Polly at ninety-six is the clearest of all; she doesn't know that it *is* past. But they all have one thing in common; they are all agreed that the story of the Millinders is the story of a family. It isn't. It's the story of a fortune.

The House of Five Talents was dedicated by its author to Florence Adèle Tobin, who died at the age of eighty-seven soon after the book appeared in print. Mrs. Tobin, the maternal grandmother of Adele Auchincloss who was named for her, was born during the same year as the fictional Augusta Millinder and, according to the dedication, freely shared her recollections with her novelist grandson-in-law. Mrs. Tobin must not, however, be seen as a "model" for Gussie, nor her family as a model for the Millinders. In 1983, nearly a quarter century after publication of *The House of Five Talents,* Auchincloss published *Maverick in Mauve,* excerpting diaries of the young Florence Adèle Sloane with sustained commentary by Louis Auchincloss himself. Descended from the Vanderbilts as well as from the Sloane family of furniture fame, Adele Auchincloss's grandmother was, unlike the awkward Gussie Millinder, one of the true beauties and socialites of her era. Married in 1895 to Adele's grandfather, James Abercrombie Burden, Jr., and after Burden's death to Richard Tobin whom she also survived, Florence Adèle Sloane emerges from her diaries as both a keen observer and an enthusiastic participant with regard to the affluent social scene of the 1890s. In retrospect, her contribution to *The House of Five Talents* would appear to lie in her vivid recollections, coupled with her encouragement as her grandson-in-law prepared to write a different kind of novel. Thereafter, Auchincloss would derive his greatest novelistic successes by focusing upon the middle distance, toward a past rendered remote and even quaint by swift transitions, yet still close enough to be remembered.

Portrait in Brownstone

Building upon the strengths inherent in *The House of Five Talents,* Auchincloss in *Portrait in Brownstone* both broadens and deepens his social and historical analysis of New York society during the first half of the twentieth century. His principal character and featured first-person narrator is one Ida Trask Hartley, a descendant of the large, close-knit Denison clan that did not cross the East River from Brooklyn into Manhattan until around the time of Ida's own birth in 1889. Although comfortably off, the Denisons have no large, inherited fortune such as the Millinders. Ida's father and uncles all work for a living, most have been to college, and one uncle, Victor Denison, is a practicing physician. Ida herself, although only sixteen years younger than the fictional Gussie Millinder, was born into a later generation, one in which women are at least "allowed," if not expected to attend college and, albeit "within limits," to develop minds and interests of their own.

For most of her sixty-odd years, the pensive, vaguely bookish Ida has stood somewhat in the shadow of her cousin, Geraldine, daughter of Dr. Victor Denison. Their rivalry, initiated by the prettier if shallower Geraldine, has lasted well into adulthood and even middle age, touching every dimension of both women's lives. Even Ida's husband,

Derrick Hartley, is disputed territory between them. Although "committed," if not engaged to Ida during 1912, Derrick fell madly and disastrously in love with Geraldine, breaking off their "understanding," yet Ida in time took him back, in part to please her terminally ailing father; in 1935, more than two decades later, the recently widowed Geraldine again intervened between Derrick and Ida, encouraging him in an extramarital adventure that she hoped would lead to his divorce from Ida and remarriage to herself.

Indeed, it is Geraldine's suicide, "so long dreaded" and often threatened, that prompts Ida to begin the first-person memoir with which the novel opens. Geraldine, after a long slide into alcoholism and depression, has jumped out the window of her small hotel apartment, itself a product of Hartley's sincere if reluctant generosity. Her death, a mixed blessing to be sure, returns Ida's thoughts to their early years as both relatives and neighbors, members of the extended Denison clan "imported" to Manhattan from Brooklyn by the prosperous broker Linnaeus Tremain who, having married one Denison, then saw fit to surround his wife with the reassuring presence of her family. Fashioned in part after the author's own Brooklyn-based Dixon relatives (*WC,* 15), the Denisons, even as they differ and disagree among themselves, are a close-knit and formidable lot, forever an enigma to such in-laws as Linnaeus Tremain and his eventual partner Derrick Hartley.

By dint of his considerable earned wealth and social position, Linnaeus Tremain looms large in Ida's girlhood recollections. Although ever careful to distance himself from the Denisons and their many intrigues, "Uncle Linn" Tremain is in fact their prime benefactor, helping them all to maintain a gracious, if seldom opulent, standard of living. Well versed in the arts as in business, reared in Europe by expatriate American parents, Tremain first met the Denisons when he bought their father's Brooklyn bank, not long thereafter taking the eldest Denison daughter as his second wife. As perceptive as he is ambitious, Tremain does not meet his true match until Derrick Hartley arrives from Boston determined to create for himself a position in Tremain's distinguished firm.

A preparatory-school classmate of Charley Tremain, Linnaeus's son by his previous marriage, Derrick Hartley has long since chosen Linnaeus Tremain as his mentor in the arts of brokerage and private banking. By the time Derrick turns up on Wall Street in search of his fortune, he has spent five years in a Boston brokerage firm to groom himself for the post and Charley Tremain has been dead for a decade. Derrick, like many another Auchincloss character both before and after him, is the son of a New England parson and a graduate of Harvard, a former scholarship student determined to succeed. Little deterred by Tremain's insistence that there is no opening in his firm, Derrick decides to wait the old gentleman out, seeking no other work as he quite literally "dines out" on his accumulated savings. It is at one of his many dinner parties that Derrick meets Mrs. Gerald Trask to whom he pours out his story, and he is most agreeably surprised to learn that Mrs. Trask is Tremain's sister-in-law. Hired at Tremain and Dodge through Mrs. Trask's intercession, Derrick soon finds himself invited to Denison family gatherings; there, he is invariably seated next to Mrs. Trask's daughter Ida, a Barnard College student and budding political liberal whom he repeatedly engages in impromptu debates, all the more heated from their opposing points of view. Although well aware that the assembled Denisons might be pairing him off with Ida, Derrick plainly enjoys her company and willingly behaves like a suitor until Ida, in an apparent test of her good fortune, assigns Geraldine to entertain him while she is out of town one weekend. His head abruptly turned by Geraldine's blonde glamour and "social butterfly" charms, Derrick proceeds to make quite a fool of himself, little perceiving that Geraldine and Ida, although rivals, are nonetheless closely bound by family ties. Somewhat against her better judgment, Ida will yield to family pressure and to Derrick's renewed attentions following Geraldine's marriage to one Talbot Keating; the assembled Denisons seem to agree that Geraldine is one of a kind, the sort of exotic creature over whom any man might reasonably be expected to lose his head at least once.

Although somewhat blighted from the start by the shadow of Geraldine, the Hartleys' marriage is a generally stable and successful union, thanks mainly to Ida's level-headed practicality. Their daughter Dorcas, born within a year after their marriage, is very much her father's favorite, a large, sullen, moody girl whose life and thoughts remain a mystery to Ida. Her brother, Hugo, two years younger, is as close to her mother as Dorcas is to her father, despite Ida's concern over Hugo's apparent aimlessness as he approaches middle age. Derrick, meanwhile, lives mainly for his business, having succeeded Tremain as head of the firm and considerably increased its profits, eventually removing Tremain's name from the corporate title after the latter's death.

Throughout the novel Auchincloss alternates Ida's reflective, first-person narrative with sections of third-person narrative presented from the viewpoints of Derrick, Geraldine, and the two Hartley offspring. Like Gussie Millinder, Ida Hartley is quite plausible both as character and as narrator, her testimony reflecting a gradual but definitive transformation from the role of observer and occasional victim into that of assertive participant. Geraldine's death, it appears, has at last liberated Ida from the shades and shadows of her past, allowing her to wield with full authority the power appropriate to her experience and earned social position.

Perhaps predictably, Ida Hartley's development is closely linked to the fortunes of her children. In one of the novel's major subplots daughter Dorcas finds work in a publishing house after college, proceeding headlong into a disastrous marriage with a young editor and would-be novelist; her divorce, stage-managed by Derrick, results not long thereafter in Dorcas's remarriage to her lawyer, Mark Jesmond, a man some dozen years her senior whom Derrick has persuaded to switch careers and join him in the firm. Ida, never close to Dorcas in the first place, cannot help noticing as Mark and Dorcas begin to undermine the aging Derrick's authority within the firm, much as Derrick himself had done to Linn Tremain a generation earlier. Hugo, meanwhile, appears distressingly unsettled at the age of thirty-five: Employed at an auction gallery cofounded and still partially owned by a branch of the Denison clan, Hugo has never married, spends most of his evenings at parties, and has recently embarked upon a potentially scandalous affair with a divorce-bound married woman. Liberated at last from Geraldine's embarrassing, constraining shadow, Ida acts swiftly and decisively to acquire a controlling interest in the auction gallery so as to install Hugo as its president; thus established, Hugo will provide a suitable match for a younger, marriageable distant cousin, the married woman soon to be forgotten. Following Derrick's disabling heart attack, suffered after a long-overdue confrontation with Dorcas and her husband, Ida becomes de facto head of the firm of Hartley and Dodge, keeping her daughter and son-in-law in check through Derrick's freely given power of attorney. At the start of her seventh decade Ida has thus blossomed, if belatedly, into a matriarch of neo-Roman proportions, supremely calm and confident in her exercise of considerable power. Her interventions, somewhat less quixotic than those of the meddlesome Gussie Millinder, are consequently rather more successful, deserving of Derrick's own candid admiration.

Authoritatively written, *Portrait in Brownstone* both sustains and enlarges the social chronicle begun in *The House of Five Talents,* marking also a return to the author's early concern with the delineation and development of character. Particularly notable is his success with the use of multiple-viewpoint narration: Ida, to be sure, is the only char-

acter permitted to speak for herself, in the first person; on the other
hand, few if any of the others possess sufficient lucidity or self-aware-
ness for the task. In his two subsequent novels Auchincloss would continue such experimentation with even more remarkable effect,
proceeding also to broaden the appeal of his chronicle by focusing upon
issues and institutions of general public interest.

The Rector of Justin

The private preparatory school for boys, located preferably in one of
the New England states, remains despite its British "public school"
antecedents a uniquely American institution. From the turn of the
twentieth century such schools have loomed disproportionately large
in American social, political, and cultural history, owing mainly to the
high distinction and visibility attained by many of their graduates in
business, government, and the professions. Himself a graduate of Groton, perhaps the most eminent and surely the best-known among "prep
schools," Auchincloss had long been concerned, as a novelist, with
both the realities and the perceived value of private secondary education. Without exception, one or more characters in each of his previous
novels is the product of a New England preparatory school usually
known as "Chelton." In *The Rector of Justin* the prep school moves from
the background to the center, serving as principal subject as well as
prime location. Through the life, ambitions, and accomplishments of
the fictional Frank Prescott, Auchincloss focuses directly upon the private boys' school as a sort of American hybrid, somewhat anomalous,
illegitimately born into American democracy by deliberate contact
with the British aristocracy.

Throughout *The Rector of Justin* Auchincloss derives considerable stylistic and quasi-documentary effect from the skillful use of multiple
first-person narrators, each limited in viewpoint by his or her own
perspective and prejudices. The main, unifying narrator is one Brian
Aspinwall, a frail, rather old-maidish young man who has come to
teach at Justin Martyr Academy during the eightieth year of the fabled
old headmaster's life. At first merely keeping a journal of his encounters and impressions, as well as of his own possible vocation to the
Episcopal priesthood, Brian goes on to project a full biography of Francis Prescott only to find that a number of Prescott's intimates have
already tried and failed in the attempt. Brian too will fail, for want of
the breadth of experience and temperament needed to complete his

chosen task; the book, as it stands, intersperses Brian's reflections with transcribed interviews, conversations, and, most significantly, written testimony from those others who have undertaken memoirs or biographies of Prescott. Notably absent from the assembled documentation is any word from Prescott himself; in keeping with his character as revealed, the old gentleman has committed little or nothing to paper in the course of his long, distinguished career, choosing instead to be remembered by his actions. Ironically, those actions, viewed and recorded by a variety of witnesses, provide in the end such a fragmented and inconclusive portrait as to discourage Brian Aspinwall from the completion of his project. The net result, however, is a stylistic and narrative tour de force that assembles all of Auchincloss's previously latent skills in what may well be his strongest and most accomplished novel.

Amusing if often exasperating in his limitations, the earnest Brian Aspinwall continues the tradition of the "unreliable" narrator used by Marquand most successfully in *The Late George Apley* (1937), rather less so in *H.M. Pulham, Esquire* (1941) and *Melville Goodwin, U.S.A.* (1951). Unsure of his own identity as well as of the future, unsettled by the outbreak of a second world war in which he is medically unfit to serve, Brian at first sees in Prescott an exemplar of the strength and conviction that he himself personally lacks. Delving deeper, however, Brian uneasily discovers the old man's gathering convictions of personal failure, convictions supported by mounting evidence that Prescott's lifelong dream of the perfect, "unique" boy's preparatory school, a dream sustained at a tremendous cost in interpersonal relationships, has after fifty years resulted in an institution little different from others of the same type. The problem, of course, is that Prescott's "dream" has been flawed from the start: Early in their acquaintance, Prescott frankly admits to Brian his amazement that Justin, in its graduates, appears to be yielding the same "product" as Endicott Peabody's Groton:

Cotty Peabody is a great man, in his way. What I really resent is that my graduates are not more different from his. For all my emphasis on the Humanities and his on God, we both turn out stockbrokers!

What Prescott does not see, and what Brian only dimly glimpses, is the fundamental irony implicit in attempting to foster "democratic" ideals in an institution with high tuition charges and a selective ad-

missions policy. Like many another New England headmaster, Prescott
as a young man prepared for his mission at Oxford, closely observing
the British public school system at work yet never perceiving the basic
incompatibility of British aristocratic ideals with the ingrained democratic ones of his own New England boyhood; for more than half a
century, moreover, he has single-mindedly drawn his double inspiration from holy Scripture and the U. S. Constitution, little mindful,
despite his considerable erudition, that both documents lend themselves to conflicting and often contradictory interpretations. Only in
his old age does Prescott finally discover the extent to which his most
trusted benefactors and trustees have kept him in ignorance about certain of their own activities and motivations, reluctant to risk shattering
a dream from which they themselves continue to draw inspiration.
Prescott's life, meanwhile, has been so thoroughly devoted to pursuit
of his vocation that he has severely slighted his family and friendships
in the process.

The basic facts of Prescott's early years are presented through the
"memoir" of Horace Havistock, his friend and classmate at one of the
earlier, prototypical New England preparatory schools. Born, like Havistock, in 1860, "Frank" Prescott was orphaned at an early age by the
death of his father in combat at Chancellorsville, followed soon after
by that of his mother. The boys' school, implies Havistock, thus became for Prescott a kind of surrogate family, inspiring his boyhood
dream of a "perfect" school for the benefit of later generations. With
the implied promise of an eventual teaching post, Prescott persuaded
the sybaritic, dilettantish Havistock to join him at Oxford as he "did
his homework" for the founding of his model school. While at Oxford,
however, Prescott appeared to lose his religious faith upon close contact
with the classics; he had never, in any case, looked forward to the
theological training deemed necessary for the running of a church-re-
lated school. Returning with Havistock to the United States in 1881,
his dream apparently abandoned, Frank Prescott found a job with the
New York Central Railroad and rose rapidly within its ranks, apparently destined for leadership and possibly diplomacy or politics. For all
his professed loss of faith, however, Prescott had never discontinued
his regular readings of Scripture, and the time came when his old vocation returned with a vengeance in what he saw as a vision, inspiring
him to abandon both his railroad career and his impending marriage
to the vivacious young Californian Eliza Dean. It was while at Harvard
in reluctant pursuit of his required divinity degree that Prescott met

Harriet Winslow, the well-derived, well-read fellow Bostonian to whom he would remain married until her death nearly sixty years later.

From the point of his marriage onward, Prescott's biography merges inextricably with the history of Justin Martyr Academy. Within twenty-five years after its founding, the school has attained enviable size and status, thanks in large measure to the efforts of David Griscam who, like Havistock before him, has attempted his own life of Prescott. Griscam, dissuaded by Prescott early in life from a career of teaching at Justin, has since become an eminent Wall Street lawyer; before he turned thirty, Griscam joined the Justin board of trustees at Prescott's invitation and has remained in that capacity ever since, handling the intricacies of fund-raising and, in general, serving as an intermediary between an idealistic Prescott and the ruder world "outside." As revealed through his "notes" and the memoir of his late son Jules also included in the novels, David Griscam is at least as enigmatic and inscrutable a man as Prescott, with a similar disregard for family and friends. By turns ruthless and pragmatic, quite capable of sharp practice and even of lying to his mentor, Prescott, for the latter's own perceived good, Griscam nonetheless cherishes his own ideal of Justin which, although different from Prescott's, is no less autocratic. Jules Griscam, in fact, will blame his doomed, rebellious existence upon his father's devotion to Justin and its headmaster, even hinting at an unhealthy passion on his father's part; by the time David Griscam approaches old age, his devotion to both man and school has become less a passion than a habit, with a strong undercurrent of resentment.

The third and youngest of Prescott's daughters, ironically and deliberately named Cordelia by her father, who no doubt wanted a son, bears eloquent if at times excessive witness to Frank's cavalier treatment of his entire family. Interviewed by a reluctant Brian in her New York apartment, surrounded by masterworks of modern art, Cordelia Prescott Turnbull is a failed painter-turned-collector with the aid of a generous settlement from her second ex-husband; she is also a plainspoken, hard-drinking Bohemian whose pronounced nymphomaniacal tendencies, in one of the novel's few truly comic scenes, send the callow Brian fleeing for dear life before their scheduled interviews can be completed. By her own accounting Cordelia is no more resentful of Prescott than either of her sisters; she is simply more articulate, having learned to express her grievances through years of psychoanalysis. Cordelia's primary grievance with her father concerns the latter's high-handed treatment of one Charley Strong, a Justin alumnus and mortally wounded World War veteran with whom she shared a brief idyll in Paris following the inevitable collapse of her first marriage: Arriving unannounced in Paris with Cordelia's mother, Prescott proceeded to exercise his old, godlike, headmasterly control over Charley, directing Charley's thoughts toward God and away from Cordelia in the process. So efficient was Prescott's therapy that Cordelia was in Italy when Charley finally died, having burned the manuscript of his novel at his old headmaster's urging. Thereafter, Prescott heavy-handedly stage-managed an annulment of Cordelia's marriage to the Roman Catholic who had refused her a divorce in time to permit her marriage to Charley. Her second husband, a self-made industrialist, was soon co-opted by her father; although a stranger to private education, Guy Turnbull soon became one of Justin Martyr's more generous benefactors, thus cementing a working friendship with Prescott that has long survived Guy's marriage to Cordelia. Through Cordelia's testimony, as through the memoir of the suicidal Jules Griscam, the reader clearly sees the dark side of the Prescott's ostensibly inspirational behavior; so too does Brian Aspinwall as he comes to question the validity of his project. Notwithstanding, Brian will complete his own theological education by war's end, uneasily tracing the old master's footsteps as he settles into a teaching career following Prescott's death.

Despite its loose structure and general lack of plot, *The Rector of Justin* is unquestionably the strongest and most enduring novel ever written on the subject of an American boarding school, deriving no small measure of its strength from the author's skillful handling of irony and ambiguity. The novel's dominant theme, underscored by its narrative structure, is the elusive nature of human "truth," necessarily relative as well as subjective: If the "truth" continues to elude Prescott, so also does it elude Brian and his fellow chroniclers, suggesting the inevitable moral blindness in all human endeavor. At the same time, the possible virtues of such a school as Justin Martyr continue to shine through the narrative, suggesting that Prescott's vision, however absurd or unrealistic, is not without its discernible merits. For all its implicit tough-minded, clear-headed criticism of American private education, *The Rector of Justin* is in no sense an exposé, even less a denunciation; rather, it is the credible account of a durable American institution caught and portrayed in all its ambiguity.

In a published address entitled "A Writer's Use of Fact in Fiction," Auchincloss deals at some length with his approach to recent history in *The Embezzler* and *The House of the Prophet*. A decade earlier, in *A Writer's Capital*, he had convincingly identified the real-life model for

Prescott as Judge Learned Hand, if only to forestall a widespread belief that Prescott represented Endicott Peabody, founder and headmaster of Groton which he himself attended. In the later address Auchincloss becomes even more specific, elaborating upon the methods with which, as a novelist, he transforms fact into fiction. Of *The Rector of Justin* he says:

Here I set myself the task of examining the effect on private eastern seaboard education of the great headmasters of the New England boys' schools in the era that ended with World War II. I gave myself the homework tasks of reading all the privately printed biographies of the gentlemen in question. I discovered that they all had striking things in common: intense religiosity, admiration (if qualified) of the British public schools, strong Puritanism and, almost always, what in the military is called command presence. I decided to take the dates and certain facts of the career of my old headmaster at Groton, Endicott Peabody, but I could not use his personality, which was too highly individual for my purpose. What I needed properly to dramatize the problems that such a man would have faced was an almost morbid doubt and a mordant intellectualism. What I found I could use, at last, were some of the qualities of Judge Learned Hand. I even borrowed some of the stories that he had told me. The whole device worked well for my purpose, and until I discussed the matter publicly it was picked up by no one but the ever-watchful Archibald MacLeish.[1]

Whatever the sources of his inspiration, Francis Prescott remains among Auchincloss's most credible and memorable characters, and the novel itself as a highly impressive exercise in fictionalized social history. For the first time in his career Auchincloss appeared to be approaching the elusive frontier that separates the novel of manners from the so-called political novel; arguably, although it deals with a school and not with a state or nation, *The Rector of Justin* is indeed a political novel, dealing with the exercise of power, with the interaction of character and compromise. In his subsequent novel, *The Embezzler,* Auchincloss would approach even more closely the traditional domain of the political novel, showing how history can be, and often is, altered for the most personal and trivial of reasons by the behavior of persons in positions of authority and public trust.

The Embezzler

For *The Embezzler,* as for *The Rector of Justin,* Auchincloss drew freely upon documentary sources and recalled events, altering the facts to suit his artistic purposes. Later in the article cited above, Auchincloss explains that what interested him about the notorious Richard Whitney case was the nature of the deed, and not the doer. Recalling his observation of the Wall Street response to the Whitney scandal, Auchincloss then goes on to cite his careful study of the relevant documents, concluding:

When I was sure I had my crime exactly right, I invented an entirely new criminal and gave him an entirely new family, plus an entirely new motivation. In this case the crime was the thing; the criminal was less important. There were plenty of types who could have committed it. I had no need to use Richard Whitney himself.

As In *The Rector of Justin,* Auchincloss in *The Embezzler* derives considerable artistic and quasi-documentary effect from the use of multiple first-person narrators, revealing character through selective observation. In a sense, his use of the technique, although here perhaps less ambitious, is even more effective than in his previous novel: The number of narrators is limited to three, and the story they tell is essentially the same, invested with fresh interest by the blindness and insight of their differing perspectives. As in *The Rector of Justin,* human "truth" is highly subjective, at times maddeningly elusive, suggesting the basic futility of any serious attempt to explain or interpret human history.

The Embezzler begins with the memoir of Guy Prime, the title character, written during 1960 to "set the record straight" for future generations. Ostensibly "revealed" following Guy's death in Panama during 1962, his narrative is followed by those of his nemesis and former friend, Rex Geer, and of Guy's ex-wife Angelica, long since remarried to Rex. Alternately perplexed and stung by Guy's interpretations of their recalled behavior and his own, Rex and Angelica undertake to set the record even straighter with recorded memoirs of their own. If there is a flaw in the basic structure of the novel (and perhaps there is not), it is that Rex and Angelica have access to Guy's narrative whereas he did not have access to theirs. Notwithstanding, *The Embezzler* remains a highly impressive example of multiple-viewpoint narrative, rivaling and perhaps even surpassing *The Rector of Justin* in its virtuosity.

As Auchincloss implies in his essay, Guy Prime is indeed a character quite different from the actual perpetrator of the crime with which he is charged in the novel. Descended from an eighteenth-century diarist and auctioneer, more recently from an Episcopal bishop of New York, Guy Prime grew up as the son of the one Prime brother who married not for money but for love. With Guy's future in mind, the elder Prime was careful not to ask money or favors of his brothers until it was time to establish Guy in his own brokerage firm, with a seat on the stock exchange; as his father had cleverly foreseen, the favor was quickly and willingly granted. Guy, in the meantime, had finished Harvard and served a brief apprenticeship at the de Grasse banking firm before departing on a tour of Europe, where he met and married the attractive, quick-witted Angelica Hyde.

From his own memoir, as from those of Angelica and Rex, Guy Prime emerges as a born salesman, even-tempered and ingratiating, intelligent but superficial. Easy and disarming of manner, well versed in all the social graces, Guy makes it his business from his earliest youth onward to keep people happy, little mindful of the resentment that his well-intentioned intrusions might breed. Like such female Auchincloss characters as Gussie Millinder, Guy is an inveterate meddler, yet, being male, he has both the authority and the leverage to impose his will upon others, at least for a while. Indeed, it is Guy's meddlesome streak that causes most of the problems in his long, stormy friendship with his Harvard classmate Reginald Geer, known familiarly as Rex.

Keen of mind and reserved of manner, Rex Geer belongs to a type that had long since become a staple in Auchincloss's fiction; like Derrick Hartley and others before him, Rex is the son of a New England parson and, thanks in part to Guy's ministrations, a graduate of Harvard. Quite probably drawn together by the proverbial attraction of opposites, Guy and Rex initially complement each other, each supplying what the other lacks, yet it is not long before each man's innate egotism will pull them toward opposite poles, preparing for the estrangement and eventual confrontation of their middle years that will have worldwide repercussions. Indeed, the gregarious Guy may well have been drawn to Rex at Harvard precisely because the latter resisted his hail-fellow charms; in any case, it was Guy who soon thereafter intervened to assure scholarship aid for Rex, who was about to leave Harvard for financial reasons. It is also Guy who introduces Rex to his lifelong employer, Marcellus de Grasse, the Primes' summer landlord at Bar Harbor; de Grasse will hire both young men as they leave Harvard, but only because Guy has shown uncharacteristic discernment in choosing Rex as his friend!

At de Grasse, it soon becomes clear that Guy, although moderately successful, is not truly "cut out" for banking. Assured of his uncles' financial backing, Guy invites Rex to join him in the brokerage firm that he is planning to establish, with Rex as a full partner in charge of banking and investment operations; he is both surprised and hurt when Rex, for the first time, refuses to go along with his plans. What Guy critically fails to perceive is Rex Geer's own pride, his need to succeed without feeling indebted; what is more, Rex has already formed a corporate loyalty to the de Grasse firm that Guy can neither share nor comprehend. There is also the matter of Rex's recent infatuation with Guy's cousin Alix Prime, an enigmatic and deeply disturbed young woman whom neither man really understands; Guy's heavy-handed, ultimately disastrous efforts at matchmaking between his friend and his cousin have damaged their friendship far more than he suspects. Rex, increasingly capable of resisting his friend's blandishments, will again refuse when Guy invites him on a tour of Europe that would oblige him to quit his job as Guy has done: By the time Guy returns from his trip to found the firm later known as Prime King Dawson & King, he has already married Angelica Hyde in Paris, with Rex Geer as his best man.

Although Guy and Rex will remain friends until their definitive rupture during 1936, relations between them grow increasingly formal, even strained, with the onset of full maturity. During World War I both men will serve as officers, yet the difference in their service will in time divide them even further: Guy, among the first to volunteer, is soon attached to General Pershing's staff despite his willingness to serve in the trenches; Rex, after deferring his service due to the pressures of his job, is sent to the front lines and emerges a hero, having destroyed an enemy machine-gun nest right before the armistice. Ever thereafter, Guy will envy Rex the latter's combat experience, while Rex remains persuaded that Guy could have seen combat had he wished to. During the following decade the two men, although they do business together, are further divided by the nature of their jobs. By Guy's own reckoning his own decade was that of the 1920s, the age of deals and speculation; Rex's decade would come later, after the crash of 1929, when a banker's conservative instincts were needed to save whatever might remain. Significantly, it is in the depths of the Depression that the two men arrive at their perhaps-inevitable confrontation.

As a salesman and trader by nature, Guy Prime is ill prepared for the retrenchment of the Depression years; having suffered few losses himself, he continues his adventurous speculations, investing in such then-risky ventures as prefabricated housing and tranquilizer pills. In his seventies Guy wryly reflects that others have since made millions from his erstwhile investments, but at the time they were risky indeed, rendering Guy especially vulnerable to the legal problems of his Georgia phosphate mine and the hurricane that destroyed his planned Caribbean resort. In order to keep his various ventures afloat, Guy borrows to the limit from a variety of institutions, proceeding thereafter to pledge securities that he holds in trust for members of his family as well as for the Glenville country club, of which he is founder and chief guiding spirit. Among the novel's more intriguing yet unresolved questions is the connection, if any, between Guy's reckless speculations and the gradual unraveling of his marriage, highlighted by Angelica's affair with Rex Geer during several months of 1934. All three narrators agree, in any case, that Guy did not begin borrowing heavily from Rex or his firm until after discovering or at least suspecting that Rex had become his wife's lover.

The focal point of the action occurs during the spring of 1936, when Guy is asked to produce some bonds that he holds in trust for the Glenville Club in preparation for a merger with a small beach club that would give Glenville members access to frontage on Long Island Sound. For the first time Guy begins to face the prospect of prosecution and imprisonment, since half of the bonds are held by de Grasse as collateral for one of Guy's many personal loans. After considerable deliberation, including consultation with his ex-mistress Angelica, Rex Geer agrees to cover the debt out of his own pocket, but only on condition that Guy liquidate his firm and retire from the market altogether, the better to protect a trusting and unsuspecting public. Left with little choice, Guy grudgingly agrees to the condition, asking only that he be given until summer's end to set his affairs in order. Rex reluctantly grants the extension, doubly bound to Guy by the fact that his son is engaged to Guy's daughter; soon Guy is trading more recklessly than ever, ostensibly in an effort to save his highly respected firm. A subsequent shortfall, twice as great as before, results in yet another appeal to Rex and a by now predictable refusal; the last loan to Guy has exhausted Rex's personal funds, and a rescue through de Grasse would implicate Rex and his firm even further in Guy's illegal activities. Guy's firm thus goes into bankruptcy and Guy himself to prison, willingly and almost happily. A subsequent hearing before the Securities and Exchange Commission, in which Guy is called as a witness, results at last in the imposition of long-threatened, long-dreaded federal controls upon the stock market, thus altering the course of American social and economic history.

Writing from the vantage point of nearly twenty-five years, the aging Guy Prime chooses to see himself, if not as a victim, at least as a scapegoat, as the man who happened to get caught with his hand in the till at a time when the Roosevelt administration was impatient to seize control of the market and could hardly wait for an excuse. Although he rather happily plays the role of buccaneer, even of stage villain, Guy persistently refuses to concede the criminality of his act, seeing it as a mere extension of sharp business practice, with the result that he will feel betrayed for life by Rex, who stole not only his wife but also his good name.

Ironically if predictably, Rex Geer sees himself and his profession, not Guy or his firm, as victims of betrayal. Speaking also on behalf of the public, Rex maintains even in his old age that Guy Prime through his actions betrayed an entire way of life, allowing the statutes of a hostile government to supplant what had hitherto been self-regulated by a gentlemanly code of honor. Notwithstanding, Rex Geer ruefully concedes that Guy's memoir, coming as late as it did, might well suffice to clear his name for posterity.

Angelica Hyde Prime Geer, whose testimony closes the novel, attributes Guy's criminality to a kind of mythomania that, she claims, characterized his entire life: Although generous by nature, Guy was given to extremes of self-aggrandizement and hero worship, investing the most ordinary persons and events with heroic disproportion. As a result, he tended in time to lose contact with reality, inhabiting a romanticized domain largely of his own making. Thus does she account for the eventual failure of their marriage, with multiple infidelities on Guy's part preceding her single affair with Rex; thus also does she explain Guy's reckless, even suicidal courting of financial and professional disaster, culminating in his almost gleeful admission of guilt as he prepared himself for prison.

Reared mainly in Europe by a well-to-do expatriate mother, Angelica stands out in sharp contrast to either of her husbands; her birthright, Roman Catholicism, for example, is equally at odds with Rex's bedrock Congregationalism and Guy's hereditary Anglicanism. Perceptive, well-read, and intelligent, Angelica is the sort of woman who, in a later time, might well have defined herself through college and career. Instead she responds to Guy's increasing infidelities with an understanding whereby she will devote all of her energies to building and maintaining their estate, Meadowview, and its riding stables, while Guy devotes his to the establishment and expansion of "his" Glenville Club; the understanding has been in force for approximately ten years when Rex, on the advice of his doctors, takes up horseback riding with Angelica as his tutor, the event which leads to their affair. Strongly rooted in true affinity and friendship, the affair lasts only a few months before Rex returns contritely to his arthritic wife Lucy, to remain faithful until her death. A brief reconciliation with Guy finds Angelica most reluctantly pregnant in her middle forties, despite Guy's predictable male jubilance; her subsequent miscarriage while riding, which might or might not have been an accident, completes her estrangement from Guy, coinciding with the latter's most reckless plunge into speculative trading. Divorced from Guy at his own request following his release from prison, Angelica will marry Rex within a year after Lucy Geer's death in 1948.

Like *The Rector of Justin, The Embezzler* is highly effective both as fiction and as social chronicle. The atmosphere of the 1930s in particular, is rendered in vivid and credible detail, lending an air of authority and authenticity to the portrayal of Guy's crime and its socioeconomic impact. Ironically, the mere existence of such a novel tends to bear out the basic premise of Guy Prime's argument: The crime that "sold out" Wall Street to the New Deal could in fact have been committed by anyone, be he Richard Whitney or Guy Prime, and would no doubt have been committed by someone, sooner or later. Indeed, the time was quite probably overdue for social and political transition, given the irrevocable economic changes already wrought by the Depression and its aftermath. The novel's multiple-viewpoint narrative, meanwhile, underscores the essential inaccessibility of "truth," even to those historians who would seek it most assiduously.

A World of Profit

After *The Rector of Justin* and *The Embezzler,* Auchincloss's fifth and last novel of the 1960s was bound to come as something of a disappointment. Narrated in the generally affectless third-person style of *Venus in Sparta* or *Pursuit of the Prodigal, A World of Profit* recalls Auchincloss's earlier novels in other ways as well: Set mainly in the 1960s despite occasional flashbacks to the 1930s, *A World of Profit* deals in depth and in detail with the postwar business "world," its clandestine transactions and quick if risky profits; the "world" is, indeed, the same one that threatened Timothy Colt, one in which Guy Prime might well appear an innocent or at least an amateur.

Its credibility somewhat hampered by characters drawn a bit too close to stereotype, *A World of Profit* ventures to explore the conflicts and contrasts between old and new business practice and their respective practitioners. Jay Livingston né Levermore, a highly successful real-estate speculator of Jewish origins only partially disguised, is cast as exemplar of the new breed; representing the old is the shabbily genteel Shallcross family, headed by an aging jurist who, despite true erudition and a strong personality, has perpetually missed his chance for legislative or diplomatic greatness. Judge Shallcross's only son, Martin, intelligent but indecisive, was Jay Livingston's classmate at Columbia and Jay has known the family ever since, alternately fascinated and repelled by the way of life they represent. Snubbed as a student by the beautiful, vain Elly Shallcross, elder of Martin's two younger sisters, Jay Livingston becomes involved with their delicate, possibly neurotic younger sister Sophie some two decades later, as he prepares to purchase the ancestral Shallcross property for one of his development projects.

Reminiscent at times of *The Cherry Orchard,* at others of *The Great Gatsby, A World of Profit* often seems too derivative to attain full credibility. Jay's romantic attentions, shifting in time from the shy, unhappy Sophie to the unhappily married, still attractive Elly, are complemented by his business machinations, eventually involving the entire Shallcross clan in severe financial risk with the imminent threat of scandal. Martin Shallcross, typecast as a weakling from the start, will commit suicide as he faces the double prospect of Jay Livingston's criminal indictment and his own inevitable bankruptcy. Elly, although perhaps in love with Livingston, will in the end lack the courage of her convictions; Sophie, teetering on the edge of another nervous breakdown, will in all likelihood be saved by the emerging love of Hilary Knowles, an affable scholar and poet who has been secretly in love with her for years. Jay Livingston, although ruined and disgraced, will nonetheless survive, no doubt to found another business empire; as resilient as he is ruthless, he has long since learned the art of putting his losses behind him.

For all its resonances of Chekhov and Fitzgerald, however, *A World of Profit* falls far short of tragedy, never truly rising above bathos. Like *Venus in Sparta, A World of Profit* is hampered not only by the general bleakness of its tone but also by the almost unrelieved banality of its characters; even Livingston, the flashy, dashing arriviste, is curiously devoid of true luster compared to such earlier Auchincloss buccaneers as Guy Prime and even Derrick Hartley. The decade of the 1960s thus ends on a curiously disappointing note, incidentally announcing the competent, polished, but generally unremarkable performance that would characterize most Auchincloss novels written after 1970. Only in *I Come as a Thief* (1973), *The House of Prophet* (1980), and *Watchfires* (1982) would Auchincloss even come close to the virtuoso performances of *The Rector of Justin* and *The Embezzler,* and then only through frank imitation of his own earlier style. During the 1970s Auchincloss's greatest successes appeared to lie in the domain of short fiction, and in his occasional fusion of short and long forms in such volumes as *The Partners* (1974), which can profitably be read either as an episodic novel or as a collection of interrelated short stories.

In retrospect, there appears little room for doubt that *The Embezzler* completes the author's basic literary statement, the body of work that constitutes his greatest accomplishment and upon which his reputation is most likely to stand.

Chapter Five

Privilege, Responsibility, and Power

Manners, Motivation, and Mobility

During the 1960s Auchincloss no doubt owed his growing popular success to his authoritative portrayal of "how the other half lives," to his authentic presentation of manners and morals behind the scenes of power. It must be noted, however, that such popular success had been preceded by at least a decade of increasing critical esteem, based mainly upon the author's lucid prose style and his unquestionable skill in delineating human character. Although frequently faulted by reviewers for confining his exposition and analysis to too narrow a segment of American life, Auchincloss nonetheless drew praise for his credible portraits of those persons and types who, for good or for ill, have through their actions and decisions left an indelible stamp upon the cultural institutions of the United States.

As Auchincloss observes in his discussion of Marquand and O'Hara (see Chapter 1), increased social mobility has moved the American novel of manners perhaps inevitably in the direction of the psychological, both in tone and in focus. Just as Marquand's Charley Gray will discover, in his middle forties, that the social distinctions shaping his life have existed largely in his mind, so also will Auchincloss's featured characters tend to define themselves in relation to perceived social patterns and structures that may, or may not, have any basis in reality. For all their close observation of manners, even such early efforts as *Sybil, A Law for the Lion,* and *The Great World and Timothy Colt* tend strongly toward psychological portraiture, as do Auchincloss's long and short fictions of the 1960s and thereafter.

Filtered through a consciousness well versed in history and literature, Auchincloss's portraits are invariably both credible and memorable, situating his characters against the broader background of Western civilization in general. Of particular interest throughout his work is the hybrid, problematical concept of an American aristocracy, most fully explored in *The House of Five Talents* and *The Rector of Justin*. Challenged early in the twentieth century by the rise of an industrious, well-educated, native meritocracy, Auchincloss's self-styled hereditary aristocrats will be obliged to test their mettle in the marketplace, most often in the banks, brokerage houses, and law firms of Wall Street. The ensuing contest resembles less a class conflict than free competition among well-matched individual personalities of whom only the fittest and most adaptable—on both sides—will survive.

Aristocracy, Meritocracy, and Ministers' Sons

The Kips always boasted that their blood was the finest in New York. They had managed to restrict it, since the eighteenth century, to the small group of families that had then been considered Manhattan society. The temptation to wade out, as the sand dried, into the endless waves of new fortunes that lapped the city had been sternly resisted. A Kip lady had been denied to a nephew of Mayor Hone in the 1830's and a Kip gentleman to a Gould heiress half a century later. Even Standard Oil would not do for the Kips, even the House of Morgan. There had been a now legendary Miss Kip, not blessed in looks or fortune, who seated alone at a ball had rejected the proferred introductions of her hostess, saying "Thank you so much, but I'm perfectly happy sitting here and thinking what everyone in this room would give for one drop of my old Kip blood!" The Kips wanted to be left alone, and their wish had been gratified. ("The Deductible Yacht," *Powers of Attorney,* 1963)

Although somewhat exaggerated for satirical effect in the above paragraph, the notion of an indigenous American aristocracy, fostered and developed by the most prosperous among the early settlers, continued to persist well into the twentieth century. By the middle of the nineteenth century, even the notorious "robber barons" had entrenched themselves as members of the aristocracy, at least when perceived from "below," and by the turn of the current century, not a few such families had further enhanced their supposed standing through intermarriage with authentic if impoverished descendants of the European aristocracies. In *The House of Five Talents* both Gussie Millinder's sister Cora and their cousin Gwen have combined, through their choice of husbands, the apparent advantages of old-world nobility and new-world purchasing power. Even without such intermarriage, both newly rich families like the Millinders and older, impoverished families like the Kips continued to foster and perpetuate the myth of blood and breeding in imitation of titled Europeans; in further imitation, they tended with time to send their sons to schools like Prescott's Justin Martyr Academy in "preparation" for eventual attendance at Harvard, Yale, or Princeton.

By the first decade of the twentieth century, when Guy Prime and Rex Geer first met as classmates at Harvard, a genteel, quasi-aristocratic background such as Guy's no longer sufficed to guarantee wealth or success: Increasingly, even the sons of the rich were required to work for a living, and a college degree was fast becoming a prerequisite for advancement in the business world. Inevitably, from college onward, well-favored young men like Guy would find themselves in competition with bright, industrious scholarship students like Rex, who would quickly acquire through their merits and performance the advantages hitherto reserved for, or at least claimed by, the hereditary aristocracy. It is surely no accident that Rex Geer, like George Dilworth, Henry Knox, and Derrick Hartley before him (not to mention countless others in Auchincloss's later fiction), is portrayed as the son of an austere New Hampshire parson.

In Auchincloss's fictional universe the Protestant clergyman's son, most commonly a native of New England, looms large as the archetype of the rising meritocracy that would challenge the entrenched, self-styled New York aristocracy on its own previously undisputed turf. From the turn of the century into the 1920s and beyond, Auchincloss suggests, the minister's son proved a formidable and skilled competitor in the New York business world: As a Protestant, at least by birth and definition, with an Anglo-Saxon name and face, he did not appear to belong to a minority group and was thus easily assimilated into the upper levels of a business world already ruled by WASPs: his Ivy League education, although acquired with the help of scholarships and part-time jobs, was essentially the same as that acquired by his initially more fortunate classmates. Typically, his born-and-bred discipline would have earned him higher grades than those of his richer friends, and an ambition fueled by memories of relative poverty would drive him toward early success. Thus did Derrick Hartley, after five years of self-imposed financial apprenticeship in Boston, arrive in New York during 1911 determined to make his mark upon the business world, and proceed thereafter to do so; thus also did the young Rex Geer discover, around the same time, his own particular talents in the arcane field of private banking. Both men would in time acquire the trappings of success, bestowed in recognition of their realized talents; by the decade of their fifties, indeed, they would be hard to distinguish from hereditary "aristocrats" like Guy, except perhaps for their continued commitment to the work ethic. Only later, after the Great Depression and a second world war, would the imaginary "gates" of Wall Street be thrown wide enough to let in the rest of the population, including non-WASPs like Jay Livingston and poor widows' sons like Timothy Colt; notwithstanding, the ministers' sons born in New England between 1880 and 1910 stand plausibly recognized as the true pioneers of the rising meritocracy, a genuine if invisible "minority" that was the first to challenge the oligarchy of American business, and not infrequently to prevail.

New York as Microcosm

Perhaps the most serious criticism leveled by reviewers against Auchincloss during his long and distinguished career is that he writes only of New York City, and then of a New York that few "real" people ever see; similarly, his featured characters, whether secure or insecure in their snobbery, are often perceived as simply uninteresting. Such criticisms, however, fail to take into account the true intent of Auchincloss's sustained social chronicle, which is to offer an authoritative yet objective view of those persons and institutions that, by dint of their prominence (whether deserved or not), have helped to determine the culture that all Americans now share. No small part of the problem is that Auchincloss is a New Yorker born and bred, hence susceptible to charges that New Yorkers are aware of no other American city or town. Had he been born and reared elsewhere, he might be treated with a bit more tolerance as an always-competent, often outstanding regional novelist whose works nonetheless exert a broad appeal, as do Faulkner's Mississippi novels or Marquand's early studies of New England. Because his territory happens to be New York, Auchincloss is thus especially vulnerable to charges of smug insularity although he is ever careful to present his characters and their actions against the broader background of Western civilization.

To be sure, Auchincloss's novels and short stories are set primarily in New York City, with occasional shifts to the fashionable resorts traditionally favored by aristocracy and meritocracy alike. Moreover, most of his featured male characters have offices on Wall Street, whether bankers, lawyers, or brokers, leaving there only for some apparently "higher" calling such as public service in the nation's capital. Like most successful writers of fiction, Auchincloss understandably writes of what he knows best, yet he carefully relates his observations to the continuity of American and European history. New York, as he sees it, is in fact the American republic in microcosm, at once rebellious against, yet ever nostalgic for, its real or imagined European origins. What is more, the power traditionally and implicitly entrusted by the entire nation to the few men (and, increasingly, women) who work on Wall Street more than justifies Auchincloss's penetrating, gently satirical analysis of those persons or types of persons often perceived, with some justice, to be running the country from behind the scenes.

Like Paris and London, New York has, moreover, long been perceived as the de facto capital to which young men from the "provinces" inevitably migrate in search of fame and fortune. If Auchincloss writes exclusively about New York, it is likewise true that he does *not* write exclusively about New Yorkers; Derrick Hartley and Rex Geer, although perhaps among the less sympathetic of Auchincloss's featured characters, are nonetheless among the more dimensional and credible, thanks in large measure to their "provincial" origins. The New York setting, moreover, allows Auchincloss to test the mettle of his characters under conditions often as stressful and revealing as those of combat; the Wall Street scene, for all its implied respectability, provides the novelist with a nearly ideal crucible for the trial and development of emergent human character.

Transition: The Years between World Wars

Originally hailed as a spokesman of the "younger generation" that had seen active service during World War II, Auchincloss soon moved away from the contemporary scene, concentrating his observations mainly upon the period of his own adolescence and early maturity. In *Portrait in Brownstone, The Rector of Justin,* and *The Embezzler,* as well as in such later efforts as *The House of the Prophet* and *The Book Class,* he proves especially adept at evoking the period between world wars, particularly the 1930s. Because of wealth and position either earned or inherited, Auchincloss's featured characters feel few direct effects of the Depression, which they may well have helped to bring about; the author, however, maintains throughout his expositions a tone of nostalgia corrected and balanced with irony. By the mid-1930s, as Auchincloss recalls, the Derrick Hartleys and Rex Geers were at the height of their self-made powers, sharing the seats of power with such surviving would-be aristocrats as Guy Prime; rising directly behind them was the generation of George Dilworth and Mark Jesmond, born just after the turn of the century. Such other Auchincloss characters as Timothy Colt, Michael Farish, Reese Parmelee, and Jay Livingston were, like the author himself, just coming of age, their perceptions and future behavior to be determined at least partially by the Depression and the growing threat of another world war. When *The Embezzler* first appeared, barely thirty years after the action described, the period recalled already seemed remote, picturesque, even quaint: It is surely no accident that Angelica Prime's gracious estate, "Meadowview," is condemned during 1937 to make room for a stretch of the Northern State Parkway; the era evoked would vanish as surely and quickly as did Jay Livingston's aristocratic older cousin Florence Schoenberg, killed with her chauffeur in the high-speed wreck of her Packard town car. Although occasionally elegiac in tone, Auchincloss's evocations of the 1930s contain some of his most skillful and authoritative writing, as he gently satirizes an era that can be recalled only—if at all—with the tempered irony of hindsight.

World War II and Its Aftermath

In Auchincloss's earlier novels the featured male characters have all served, like the author himself, as commissioned naval officers during World War II; even George Dilworth, born around 1902, is credited with commissioned service in naval intelligence. For the most part, however, the characters were born between 1910 and 1920 and were just old enough to have begun their business or professional careers during the years immediately preceding the Japanese attack on Pearl Harbor. For some, like Philip Hilliard and Michael Farish, the four war years have provided a diverting break in the routine, seasoned with extramarital affairs; for others, such as Timothy Colt and Reese Parmelee, the war has been a mere bother, a loss of seniority in their rise toward promotion or partnership. For those already married, as the author himself was not, the war years also effected profound and lingering changes in the characters' relationships with their wives and young children; not infrequently, the absence of a husband during wartime would bring a wife into closer contact with her in-laws, thus placing added stress upon an already strained relationship between her husband and his parents. Whether or not the husband had strayed from his marital vows during wartime, his return to civilian life was invariably marked by the combined pressures of resuming both his marriage and his career: Reese Parmelee, perhaps the most representative of Auchincloss's early protagonists, discovers to his consternation that his wife Esther, formerly as critical as he of the prevailing "upper-class" social standards of Long Island's North Shore, has become as attached as his own mother to the perceived "value" of country clubs and boarding schools. As an associate in a law firm named in part for one of his ancestors, Reese feels increasingly out of place, rather like a reluctant actor in a play written for him by his family. To a greater or lesser degree, all of the males featured in Auchincloss's early novels share Reese's sense of maladjustment in a rapidly changing postwar world.

Dreamers, Thieves, Cads, and Bounders

The men who populate Auchincloss's fictionalized Wall Street are a varied and entertaining lot, colorful despite the dark suits that serve them almost as a uniform. A strict ethical code, honored in the breach as well as in the observance, continues to inform the working of the Street, whose offices attract opportunists and idealists in approximately equal proportion. Timothy Colt and Reese Parmelee, along with several counterparts in Auchincloss's shorter fictions, are representative idealists, spurred on to brilliant performance by a strict, perhaps excessively literal, belief in the ethical code; inevitably, their beliefs will be tested by the harsher realities of the marketplace. With the death of his honest mentor Henry Knox, Timothy Colt will "sell out" to the opposition as wholeheartedly as he has hitherto resisted it, reserving only the small spark of decency that, indirectly, will lead to his professional disgrace. Reese Parmelee, by contrast, will go to exorbitant lengths to protect his idealism, in effect encouraging both his wife and his partner to lie to him in order to keep his dream intact. Bayard Kip, the well-derived young attorney in "The Deductible Yacht," replicates Timmy Colt's crisis and reversal in condoning the sharp business practices of the Armenian-born builder Inka Dahduh; unlike Timmy, however, he will emulate Reese in closing his eyes to the obvious, accepting a partnership based mainly upon his professional relationship with Dahduh.

Unlike Timothy Colt and Bayard Kip, other Auchincloss lawbreakers are born, not made. Michael Farish, although perhaps an idealist by temperament, is fundamentally weak, given to compromise and self-indulgence. Guy Prime, at least as seen by his ex-wife Angelica, is less a criminal than a mythomaniac, hopelessly committed to his own neoromantic vision of the world. Unlike Michael Farish, Guy at least is honest with himself, his criminal behavior representing not weakness but the logical, if illegal, extension of his professional behavior. Martin Shallcross, a far less cognizant or engaging character than Guy, lapses into criminal behavior under the dominion of the flamboyant, unscrupulous Jay Livingston; his almost unwitting suicide, like that of Michael Farish, reflects a loss of control that has long been evident to everyone except possibly himself.

Tony Lowder, the male protagonist of *I Come as a Thief* (1972), is surely among the author's more intriguing if ambiguous creations, combining in his affable yet oddly driven person certain salient features of both Timothy Colt and Guy Prime. A politically inclined securities lawyer of mixed Irish-Catholic and Jewish ancestry, Tony accepts an appointment with the Securities and Exchange Commission after losing his first congressional race at the age of forty-three; his new job, intended by the Democratic Party to keep Tony in public view, also places him in plain sight of mobsters who soon manage to "reach" him through Max Leonard, his weak-willed, longtime law partner. Although personally innocent thus far of any wrongdoing, Tony is motivated by loyalty and a strange, quasi-mystical sense of guilt and expiation to share the burden of Max's involvement with loan sharks. Despite a well-earned adult reputation for probity, Tony will vividly recall a sustained episode of kleptomania during his adolescence; like Timothy Colt, Tony Lowder hankers after absolutes and will opt for public confession of his crimes, going on to testify, as does Guy Prime, before a Senate committee. To a greater degree than any of Auchincloss's Protestant heroes, Tony tends to see his checkered life and career in essentially religious terms, not unlike a wayward pilgrimage; thus motivated, he remains an irritating puzzle to his austere Protestant father-in-law, Pieter Bogardus, who for the first time in his life will violate the ethical code in an effort to destroy Tony. After all, reasons Bogardus, "How can I not hate him? A man who talks about Christ in the Down Town Association!" At the end of the novel Tony Lowder, like Timothy Colt before him, faces disbarment and an uncertain future, yet there is little doubt that he, like Timmy, will survive.

Liberation as Privilege and Vice Versa

Since the publication of *Sybil* during 1951, Auchincloss has drawn deserved praise for his credible, authoritative, and generally sympathetic portrayal of featured female characters, drawn with a skill that seems to elude the male novelists to whom he is most frequently compared. Marquand's women characters, by contrast, appear as flat, shrewish caricatures, and those of O'Hara as shrill, name-calling nymphomaniacs. Sybil Hilliard and Eloise Dilworth, in particular, bore witness to the author's concern with the emergent female consciousness, no longer content with a role predetermined by the male of the species. Although not yet "liberated" by the standards of a later generation, Eloise and Sybil are both well educated and articulate, increasingly restive under the double standard implied in their marriage vows. Ann Colt, Eileen Shallcross, and Alida Farish, although secondary characters, are all dimensionally drawn, as is Reese Parmelee's second wife Rosina; by their assertiveness, they stand out in sharp contrast to their mothers and friends, most of whom have implicitly accepted, through their behavior, the female stereotype to which the author relegates them: Julia Anderton is a typical unmarried "vamp," Flora Farish a typical married one; of Philip Hilliard's sisters only the youngest, Arlina, seems likely ever to emerge from stereotype, and Esther Means Parmelee Coit has willingly embraced the stereotype even to the point of caricature. It was not until the 1960s, however, that Auchincloss's strongest, most memorable female characters would begin to emerge, starting with the brusque, intelligent, and outspoken Gussie Millinder.

As a lifelong spinster, Miss Gussie Millinder comes to enjoy a degree of freedom and independence generally denied by society to women born during the 1870s: Left to her own devices, Gussie with the approach of middle age begins to take college courses and even to teach in a girls' school, although she has scant need of the money; her prior self-education in literature and the arts has, moreover, been far from inconsiderable. With the arrival of World War I she volunteers for auxiliary service in Europe, proceeding thereafter to define herself still further through a career of active if selective community service, giving as freely of her time as of her fortune. As she ages, she is quick to perceive the advantages that she has enjoyed over her married sister, cousins, and nieces, even as the latter tend to regard her spinster status with condescension. The true emancipation of the married American female would, Auchincloss suggests, come only later, pioneered by such belated "awakenings" as those of Ida Hartley.

During the fifteen years separating Ida Trask's maturity from that of Gussie Millinder, it had become possible, if not yet fully acceptable, for a well-bred woman to attend college; significantly, however, Ida is the first among her family and friends to do so, and she is generally considered to have "done the right thing" in dropping out of college to marry a man who had previously rejected her. True, it is not until four decades later, after Geraldine's suicide, that Ida will finally put her brains and education to good use; moreover, Ida's self-assertion, when at last it takes place, hardly amounts to "liberation" in the currently accepted sense; at most she has metamorphosed from matron into matriarch, manipulating her family from an unseen perch behind the scenes. Ida's inner transformation, however, has been far greater than her external behavior might indicate, suggesting that future generations of educated, assertive women would in fact be quicker and more decisive in taking control of their lives.

Like Gussie Millinder, Ida Trask Hartley comes to recognize the liberation born of privilege; not for another two generations, with relatively unrestricted access to professions and the workplace, would women without inherited means approach a similar level of self-determination; nor did all women similarly privileged avail themselves of the opportunities, however limited, at their disposal: Angelica Prime, although well-read, assertive, and intelligent, does not attend college; as a rich matron, spurned or ignored by Guy, she will opt for a large house with adjoining grounds and stables, eventually indulging herself in an extramarital affair with Guy's best friend.

In *The Partners,* a collection of linked short stories advertised and published as a novel during 1974, Auchincloss addressed himself directly to the issue of women's changing status and stature, both at home and in the workplace. "The Marriage Contract," among the most incisive and sharply focused of the stories, shows conflict and possible resolution between the Curriers, both practicing attorneys and employed by rival Manhattan law firms. Marcus Currier, reared with all the prejudices of his parents' generation, resents Felicia's professionalism even though it helped to form the basis of their mutual attraction, and though Marcus himself has come to depend upon her informed legal advice. "I wasn't criticizing," observes managing partner Beekman Ehninger, with glancing reference to his own wife. "I'm sure she's a mine of discretion. But it seems to one of my generation such an odd

relationship to have with one's wife. I can't conceive of Annabel reading a brief, much less writing one. But I suppose it's fun. Another way
of sharing." Significantly, both Marcus and his superior remain unper-
suaded by their mutual reassurances, although it is none other than
Ehninger who will propose the "marriage contract" of the story's title.
In the meantime, Felicia Currier will have proposed two personal-
professional arrangements to Marcus, only to meet with rejection; it is
only after he refuses to join her in a husband-wife legal partnership
that Felicia seeks employment with a Washington-based anti-pollution
lobby, inviting Marcus to join her at a substantial raise in aggregate
salary. Marcus, however, is quick to note that Felicia's salary would be
the larger, and to opt for the status quo at Shepard, Putney, and Cox
despite the inevitable threat of separation. Felicia, in turn, is non-
plussed by how easily their children adapt to her long absences, and
the time is soon ripe for such an ironically Draconian solution as the
one proposed by Beeky Ehninger.

For all Auchincloss's skill in dealing with the current generations of
supposedly "liberated" women attempting to liberate their men from
the prejudices of an earlier era, it is clear that his real interest still lies
with the women of his mother's generation, contemporaries of Angelica
Prime, Lucy Geer, and Ida Hartley. Liberation, unspoken as a word
and barely formed as an idea, was considered the exclusive province of
suffragettes and Lucy Stoners, "overeducated" political agitators hardly
noted for their femininity. Frances Ward Leitner, first wife of Felix
Leitner in *The House of the Prophet,* is both a representational and an
exceptional specimen of the breed: Born around 1890 into the upper
levels of New York society, Frances Ward nonetheless fashioned for
herself a career in law and activism, her success due in part to her
unprepossessing stature and plain, even homely appearance; in looks at
least, Frances was very much a typical bluestocking of her generation,
readily accepted among women activists of less privileged origin; yet
at the same time her family connections allowed her to function freely
and effectively at all levels of society. More typical of her generation
were the members of *The Book Class,* profiled in a 1984 fictional memoir of that title by the bachelor son of Cornelia Gallatin Gates, a charter
member. From its title onward *The Book Class* suggests a certain dilet-
tantism, a flirtation with learning unconsummated by true education:
For the most part, the members of the book class are intelligent, sophisticated, and moderately well-read, yet unwilling to face the con-

sequences of incipient, de facto liberation; the most "liberated" among them are content to meet their perceived needs by dominating or manipulating their husbands, never quite reaching the level of success achieved by Ida Hartley. One of their number, Justine Bannard, who understands her husband Chester better than he understands himself, contrives successfully to break up his latest extramarital affair by offering him his freedom; later, Justine will intervene, unseen and unsuspected, to ruin Chester's chances for returning to his old school as headmaster. The irony in both situations is that Justine's political power remains covert, little suspected by Chester for the rest of his natural life. Another member, Georgia Bristed, achieves strange notoriety as a perverse political hostess, regularly switching loyalties to whichever party or persuasion happens to be *out of* favor at the time. The prevailing impression left by *The Book Class* is one of wasted or at least misspent energy and effort; one wonders, as no doubt does Auchincloss himself, exactly what such women might have achieved had they truly felt the courage of their convictions.

In *Watchfires* (1982), set mainly during the years immediately preceding the Civil War, Auchincloss offers in the person of Rosalie Handy Fairchild one of his more memorable and intriguing feminine portraits, plausible despite the nineteenth-century setting. Although Rosalie is said to have died at fifty-four around the time Gussie Millinder was born, the circumstances of her life and career offer an arresting admixture of privilege and liberation, implicitly questioning the long subsequent delay in development of self-determination among women in the United States; here as elsewhere, Auchincloss shows his strong advocacy of feminist perspectives and causes, underlain by his implied impatience with the slowness of women to espouse their own cause.

As the wife of a Wall Street attorney and third daughter of a rich, self-made political "kingmaker," Rosalie Handy Fairchild has had ample opportunity to observe power in action, at least among the males of the species. Long aware, as her husband Dexter is not, of Dexter's strong attraction to her younger sister Annie, Rosalie involves herself deeply in the abolitionist cause just as that attraction is about to result in an affair. Dexter, ethical by nature even in his infidelity, offers Rosalie large donations in support of her undisclosed "cause," with the tacit condition that neither spouse will ask questions of the other. With the onset of war Rosalie volunteers with her elder sister for nursing service on a Union hospital ship, proceeding after the war to distinguish herself as an articulate advocate of women's suffrage. Ironically, Dexter Fairchild, despite his own patriotic instincts, never gets to share his wife's participation in the war effort; bound by an unspoken pact to his father-in-law as a consequence of his affair with Annie, Dexter will assist Charles Handy in the raising of funds, materiel, and troops for the Union cause; only after the war, as a member of the defense in the impeachment trial of President Andrew Johnson, will Dexter feel that he, too, has participated in the nation's history. Still, Rosalie will continue to outshine her husband even after death, notable for her awareness and self-definition.

Unfortunately, suggests Auchincloss, some women never learn. In "Equitable Awards," set in the early 1980s and published during 1983 as part of *Narcissa and other Fables,* Gwendolen Burrill, a lawyer's wife seeking divorce, refuses to claim her rightful share of her husband's income until her attorney, Miriam Storrs, herself a doctor's wife, calls Gwen's attention to Sidney Burrill's romantic involvement with the young female associate whom he has engaged to represent him in the divorce action. Unable or unwilling to claim her born rights as a woman, Gwen Burrill is almost too quick to claim her stereotypical rights as a "woman wronged," asserting out of spite what she has refused to claim through enlightened self-interest. Liberation, Auchincloss wryly implies, remains available only to those women—and men—actively willing to seek it.

The Neutered Narrator

With the felicitous invention of Miss Gussie Millinder, Auchincloss happened upon a narrative device that would serve him well in *The Rector of Justin* and *The House of the Prophet,* and to which he would also return in *The Book Class,* that of the unmarried observer and recorder. Unencumbered by spouse or children, often included in confidences which others are spared, the bachelor or spinster can serve as a uniquely privileged observer, also quick to pass judgment without fear of being judged in return—except as one who has not taken part in married life. Gussie, the first and perhaps the finest of Auchincloss's oddly "neutered" narrators, has observed nearly sixty years of marriage, dalliance, discord, and divorce with an increasingly jaundiced eye. In her twenties at the time of her parents' divorce and her father's remarriage to an actress, Gussie comes to value the good fortune of her spinsterhood, the better to observe, if not exactly to judge, other people's misbehavior. By 1948, a number of her relatives have experienced divorce, while most of the others remain married in name only, their unions flawed by infidelities duly noted and recorded by Gussie. In *The Rector of Justin* Brian Aspinwall functions largely as a male counterpart to Gussie, free to comment upon the marital and parental lives of others from the safe haven of his somewhat nervous bachelorhood.

In the later novels Auchincloss's use of the privileged bachelor narrator borders at times upon caricature. Roger Cutter, Felix Leitner's longtime assistant and would-be biographer in *The House of the Prophet*, has been rendered impotent for life by a diabetic crisis sustained during late adolescence; he is thus "privileged" to serve and observe Leitner's disordered marital and amatory life with the dispassion and dedication of a court eunuch, permanently immune, as Felix is not, to the charms of the ladies who move through their lives. Christopher Gates, the chronicler-narrator of *The Book Class*, is frankly if discreetly homosexual, a proclivity that affords him license to record and criticize with apparent objectivity the marital and parental misadventures of his mother's friends. Stereotypically, Chris happens to be an interior decorator by trade, the more intelligent if less handsome of two brothers. Although not the only admitted homosexual to appear in Auchincloss's novels, Chris is nonetheless the first to serve as narrator, cherishing well into his sixties his boyhood role as mascot of the book class. On balance, he is somewhat less engaging and entertaining as a narrator and memorialist than is Roger Cutter, into whose persona Auchincloss managed to combine most of the strengths and few of the weaknesses of Brian Aspinwall.

Keepers of the Keys

In *Watchfires* Auchincloss provides what may well be his fullest and most satisfactory exploration to date of a theme that underlies most of his published fiction: In Auchincloss's view, the bankers, brokers, and lawyers of Wall Street constitute a kind of secular priesthood, entrusted by an unseen public with the maintenance of law and order; thus does Rex Geer inwardly accuse Guy Prime of a treason bordering upon sacrilege; thus also does Michael Farish come to see himself as both a traitor and an outcast, unworthy by temperament of the position that should be his by birthright. Henry Knox, although a minor character, functions largely as a custodian of the public trust, with anarchy set

loose after his untimely death; Harry Hamilton, in attempting to jus-
tify or disguise his strong personal animus toward Eloise Dilworth,
will more than once represent himself as a guardian of the quasi-sacred
mysteries by which law and order are maintained. It was not until
Watchfires, however, that Auchincloss would present in depth a lawyer's
self-concept and its consequences, showing also the frequent discrep-
ancies between private person and public persona.

From his symbolic names outward Dexter Fairchild personifies the
codes and values of both his culture and his chosen profession. As the
only son of a disgraced Episcopal priest who left both church and family to elope to Europe with a married woman, Dexter has in effect
dedicated his life and career to the expiation of his father's sins, sub-
stituting the law for a priesthood in which he can no longer believe.
Even at forty, he is still half-consciously attempting to please his
wronged, ambitious mother, to whose efforts he credits much of his
prosperity and professional success. Indeed, not until his own extramarital affair, long dreaded, sublimated, and delayed, will Dexter
come to view his life and career with objectivity, proceeding thereafter
toward a true "liberation" rivaling that of his wife Rosalie.

As seen and treated by the other characters, Dexter Fairchild at the
start of *Watchfires* is dignified, reserved, even stuffy, with a tendency
toward prudishness. His adventure begins when, as self-appointed
guardian of the family honor, he undertakes to discredit one Jules
Bleeker, a journalist and man-about-town who may or may not be
having an affair with Rosalie's sister Annie, married to Dexter's bibu-
lous cousin and law partner Charley Fairchild. At first, only Rosalie
suspects the personal motivations behind Dexter's increasingly vindictive campaign; even so, she attempts to warn him against taking
himself or his role too seriously. In a passage that Dexter will long
remember, she likens his self-perceived role to that of a pagan high
priest:

But she was determined not to let him escape her, as he so often had, with
emotional formulas. "What I think I mean is this," she said firmly. "I have a
theory that men, like women, have been basically the same through history.
The majority, that is. The average Roman, the average Greek, wasn't he
pretty much like the average American today? What makes one era different
from another is its dogma, not its people. And isn't its dogma always made
up by the small, busy group we call priests?" He stared. "And I'm a priest?
Is that what you're getting at?"

It occurred to her that he did not altogether object to the idea. "Yes, a priest doesn't have to be a clergyman. He's simply a person in charge of the mysteries. Whether they're religious or political or what have you. His job is to keep the others in line. He has to use miracles and magic." She paused now, watching him carefully. "He may even have to fake them."

Only later, after Dexter has succeeded in banishing Jules Bleeker from New York, will Annie challenge Dexter to declare himself, thus inaugurating the affair so long deferred. By that time, it is clear to both Dexter and to the reader that Annie's marriage to Charley six years earlier was in fact arranged by Dexter as a pragmatic solution to his repressed infatuation with his wife's vivacious, fickle younger sister.

Disoriented by the sudden force of his emotions, Dexter will come, during and after his tempestuous interlude with Annie, to examine his life and career as if through the eyes of a stranger. To his surprise, he discovers that he has few political or social convictions of his own, having assumed without question the conservative orientation of his father-in-law and his mother. For the first time, he begins to evaluate issues objectively, especially with regard to the threat of war between the states, questioning motivations on both sides; later, during Reconstruction, he will vote his conscience rather than his class, achieving from his middle years onward a well-deserved reputation for fairness and objectivity both as lawyer and as statesman. Ironically, Dexter is still to be counted among the "high priests," although Rosalie's interpretation of the term continues to resonate in his mind as a necessary corrective to blind self-importance. From the war years onward Dexter's "priestly" status will be earned, rather than merely assumed as if by birthright.

Viewed retrospectively from *Watchfires,* the bulk of Auchincloss's fiction both long and short may indeed be seen as depicting the "keepers of the keys," the guardians of mysteries both sacred and profane. Francis Prescott's Justin Martyr Academy may, moreover, be seen as the prototypical vehicle for the transmission of such mysteries from one generation of guardians to the next, even as Prescott will deplore the mere concept of a hereditary American elite. It is in *Watchfires,* however, that Auchincloss presents his fullest exploration of the theme, showing also the dangers inherent in the confusion of person with profession.

Mobility and Mediation

Throughout his published fiction Auchincloss, as a chronicler of social structures and mobility, displays an instinctive grasp of the concept
of "mediated desire" first developed by René Girard in *Mensonge roman-
tique et vérité romanesque* (1961; *Deceit, Desire and The Novel*, 1966).
Closely familiar with most of the works and authors discussed by Girard in his study, Auchincloss had already filtered his social observations
through a well-prepared literary consciousness, often arriving as an author at conclusions similar to those reached by Girard as a critic.

In sum, Girard's complex analysis reexamines the mythic structures
of modern literature—focusing mainly on Cervantes, Stendhal, Dos-
toevsky, and Proust—to reveal the prevalence of "mediated" desire, a
sentiment similar to mere jealousy yet compounded by compulsive emulation: The object or objects of desire, be they possessions, position,
or woman viewed as possession, are rendered desirable to the subject
by the fact that someone else has them, rather than by any intrinsic
"desirability." The possessor, as "mediator" between subject and object, is simultaneously admired, emulated, and hated, ultimately
viewed as a barrier, not a link, between desired object and desiring
subject:

As the distance between mediator and subject decreases, the difference dimin-
ishes, the comprehension becomes more acute and the hatred more intense. It
is always his own desire that the subject condemns in the Other without
knowing it. Hatred is individualistic. It nourishes fiercely the illusion of an
absolute difference between the Self and that Other from which nothing separates it. Indignant comprehension is therefore an imperfect comprehension—
not nonexistent as some moralists claim, but imperfect, for the subject does
not recognize in the Other the void gnawing at himself. He makes of him a
monstrous divinity. The subject's indignant knowledge of the Other returns
in a circle to strike him when he is least expecting it. This psychological circle
is inscribed in the triangle of desire. Most of our ethical judgments are rooted
in hatred of a mediator, a rival whom we copy.[1]

To a large extent, as Auchincloss is well aware, the process of social
mobility is in fact an instance of mediated or, as Girard often calls it,
"triangular" desire, in which certain objects are coveted not for their
intrinsic worth but for their perceived value to others. Timothy Colt,
during his separation from Ann, flirts less with Eileen Shallcross than
with her life-style, experimenting with the cultural life of concerts and

museums that he perceives as the privileged enclave of the very rich. Eileen, meanwhile, functions less as object than as mediator, initially emulated, subsequently hated and repudiated. In the case of Francis Prescott, the "mediator" is the English public school and, by extension, the entire British class system: Over sixty years, Prescott will quietly plan and execute an "American revolution" of his own, little anticipating or suspecting the ultimate futility of his self-contradictory "dream." In *Watchfires* Dexter Fairchild will silently accept the mediation of his father-in-law and mother, only to rebel by replicating, in mid-life, the adulterous behavior of his disgraced and detested father. It is in *The Embezzler,* however, that the concept of triangular mediation receives its fullest and most complete expression, rendered even more complex by the mutual attraction and repulsion of two "mediators."

Early in *The Embezzler* Guy Prime recalls his father's repeated warnings about Rex Geer:

"Do you imply that he's using me?"

"Certainly he's using you, and I don't blame him in the least. These things aren't done in cold blood, mind you. The circumstances create them. You will understand that when you've watched the human antheap as long as I have. Young Geer is by nature a self-aggrandizing animal. He moves upwards wherever you put him. Of course, he'll crawl over you, if you let him. He can't help himself. He wants the moon. He wants to be first in de Grasse, first in Wall Street, first in society."

"Rex cares nothing for society," I cried indignantly.

"Rex cares for anything he hasn't got," Father said emphatically. "You think, because he doesn't enjoy things, that he doesn't want them. You're dead wrong. He may want them just because someone else has them, but he still wants them."

As the action develops throughout the multiple narratives, it becomes clear that both Guy and his father are somewhat wrong about Rex, whose actions and motivations prove to be considerably more complex than they imagine. The process of triangular mediation, however, continues to animate the action, with Guy and Rex each functioning as the other's emulated, ultimately hated mediator. Even as Rex may or may not envy Guy the latter's perceived background and social position, Guy will envy Rex's superior intellect, industry, and talent. Marcellus de Grasse, who befriended Guy as a boy, will nonetheless hire him only because of his friendship with Rex, and it is not long before Rex "outperforms" him. During World War I each man

will again serve as model and mediator to the other, all the while
detesting the other's perceived accomplishments. The inevitable conflict between entrenched "aristocracy" and rising "meritocracy" is thus
worked out at a basic, intensely personal level, with Rex eventually
"winning" through the "capture" of Guy's wife whatever might have
hitherto eluded him.

Elsewhere in Auchincloss's fiction, the practice and prevalence of
snobbery continue to illustrate Girard's concepts of triangular mediation. As an inveterate reader of Proust as well as an observer of the
social scene, Auchincloss is well aware of the imitative nature of ambition, or even of snobbery as an end in itself. Jay Livingston, even as
he deplores decay and decadence among the Shallcross family, finds
himself inevitably drawn toward what they appear to represent, just as
they are alternately attracted and repelled by the superior "vitality"
implicit in Livingston's ambition. As Girard observes in his discussion
of Proust,

The triangular structure is no less obvious in social snobbism than it is in
love-jealousy. The snob is also an imitator. He slavishly copies the person
whose birth, fortune or stylishness he envies. . . . The snob does not dare
trust his own judgment, he desires only objects desired by others. That is why
he is the slave of the fashionable.[2]

At times, as in the case of Reese Parmelee, the mediation of snobbery may be seen to operate in reverse. Due in part to his own "shel-
tered" upbringing, Reese has come to covet, or at least to desire
intensely, the supposedly simple life of "lesser" folk, and is quite non-
plussed to discover in artists, writers, and the "uptown" lawyer Amos
Levine the same pettiness and venality that he strove to put behind
him upon leaving Wall Street and Long Island; he is equally non-
plussed to discover in his second wife, Rosina, a yearning for the trappings of his former life. What Reese fails to take into account is that
Rosina's upward mobility, the quality that accounts for her success as
a journalist, is inevitably fixed upon the perceived "heights" from
which he has quite willingly "descended." Unwittingly and unwillingly, Reese by his origins will come to serve Rosina as a mediator,
thus rendering all but impossible the escape that he has worked long
and hard to effect.

In his own memorable essay on Proust published in *Reflections of a
Jacobite* Auchincloss, despite several severe and serious criticisms, ul-

timately praises the older French novelist for having successfully caught and portrayed the flexibility that, ironically and unexpectedly, is built into the structure of any self-styled "aristocracy." The simple fact of the matter, notes Auchincloss, is that those in power or control reserve the right not only to make the rules, but also to change them at will:

Most people who write about society, whether they be novelists or sociologists or simply gossip columnists, make the basic error of assuming that there must be some consistency in its standards. They take for granted that there are rules which govern the qualifications of those seeking admission, that if one has been richly born or gently born, or if one can play polo or excel at cards, or if one has the gift of pleasing or is a good shot or a good conversationalist, one may tap with confidence at any closed gates. When the rules are seen not to apply, the observer concludes that they once did, but have since broken down. As the cases of nonapplication multiply, he is apt to shrug in frustration and say, "Oh, well, nowadays, it's only a question of money!" What Proust alone had the patience to piece out is that any society will apply all known standards together or individually, or in any combination needed to include a maverick who happens to please or to exclude an otherwise acceptable person who happens not to. Nor are society people conscious of the least inconsistency in acting so. They keep no records, and have no written constitution. Why should their rules be defined in any way other than by a list of exceptions to them?[3]

If the society studied by Proust, largely populated by titled European aristocracy, freely allows itself to revise its own codes and judgments, the New York society that forms the principal subject of Auchincloss's fiction is even more likely to do so. In the United States, founded by refugees from the British class system, "arrival" is very much a relative term. Does one speak, indeed, of the arrival of one's ancestors in the New World, or of one's own "arrival" into the upper reaches of bourgeois "aristocracy" by dint of hard work, parsimony, and sheer luck? Auchincloss, throughout his novels and short stories, remains very much aware of society's shifting standards, no less arbitrary for being basically capricious. In less than forty years the penurious son of a New England preacher could, and often did, find himself at the pinnacle of both commerce and society, revered as an arbiter of taste and decorum. By the same token, the hereditary "aristocrat" could, if he so chose, simply sink into oblivion; the main reason that Reese Parmelee does not succeed in doing so is that he carries into his self-imposed exile the same energy and drive that have marked him for success in the society that spawned him. In "The Prince and the Pauper," one of the most successful stories included in *Second Chance*, Auchincloss depicts in Brooks Clarkson a member of the "aristocracy" who despite, or even because of, his exceptional intelligence and looks, manages in a few short years to effect his own disappearance from "society." Even more than Reese Parmelee, the decadent Brooks symbolizes a self-exile from society that, implies Auchincloss, is by no means uncommon.

In "The Prince and the Pauper," as the title predicts, Auchincloss balances Brooks Clarkson's declining fortunes against those of Benny Galenti, the law-school dropout whom Brooks first elevates from office boy to chief administrator in his law firm, then establishes as a rich, self-made investor. At the end of the story, after Brooks Clarkson's deliberate slide into unemployment and alcoholism, Benny Galenti will still attempt to defend his former benefactor against charges leveled by Clarkson's own cousin, Byron Fales:

Benny watched grimly as those thick, facile hands busied themselves with the bottles and glasses massed in the center of the table. "Make me comfortable, by all means. But there's still something I don't see. How can Brooks be decadent and creative at the same time?"

"What do you suggest he has created?"

"Me."

"Oh, come off it, Benny. Just because he loaned you some dough in a tight spot doesn't mean . . ."

"Now listen to me, Byron. It was Brooks who singled me out of the office boys in his firm and pushed me ahead. It was Brooks who sold me to his partners as office manager. It was Brooks who got me to move to Glenville and loaned me the money to buy Xerox. It was Brooks . . ."

"Well, if he's so damn creative, why didn't he buy Xerox himself?"

"Because that isn't his way."

"He could have, couldn't he?"

"I suppose."

"But he'd rather watch, is that it? He's rather sit back and gaze into his man-making machine? Do you know that you've just proved the very point you were trying to rebut? You've described the most decadent creature that ever drew a fetid breath!"

Benny Galenti, by the time of the quoted conversation a member of the Glenville Club founded by Guy Prime, will in time, it is assumed, rise through his efforts and good fortune to the upper reaches of Long Island society. His Italian name and origins will by that time have been accepted; meanwhile, the prevailing yet changing social code will forbid him ever to mention, or perhaps even to remember, the name and person of ex-attorney Brooks Clarkson. Society will continue to protect its own, but only by invitation; at the same time, invitations can be canceled and welcomes outworn. Auchincloss, in praising Proust's observations concerning social flexibility and mobility, has clearly committed himself also to learning Proust's lesson well.

Chapter Six

The Novel as Omnibus: Auchincloss's Collected Short Fiction

Auchincloss and Short Fiction

Although deservedly best known for his novels, Auchincloss since the later 1940s has earned acclaim also as a writer of incisive, memorable short stories. In his first two published collections, *The Injustice Collectors* (1950) and *The Romantic Egoists* (1954), the stories are thematically linked; in certain subsequent collections, such as *Powers of Attorney* (1963), *Tales of Manhattan* (1967), and *The Partners* (1974), the collected stories are linked through recurrent characters as well. In those volumes Auchincloss appears to be attempting a fusion of short and long fiction with stories that can be read either individually or in sequence, offering the double satisfactions of the short story and the novel. *The Partners,* in fact, was originally advertised and published as a novel, although it is little different in form and structure from the earlier *Powers of Attorney. The Winthrop Covenant* (1976) attempts a family saga of sorts through a chronological series of short fictions; *Narcissa and Other Fables* (1983) is basically a traditional collection of shorter pieces, some of them very short indeed. In *The Book Class,* published the following year as a novel, Auchincloss again combines the conventions of short and long fiction, although rather less successfully than in *Powers of Attorney* or *The Partners*: Although episodic in form, *The Book Class* has the outward structure of a novel, demanding that it be read from start to finish, not piecemeal; at the same time, the action remains too loosely plotted to deliver the satisfactions normally expected of the novel. Notwithstanding, *The Book Class* remains noteworthy as an example of his continued experimentation with the fusion of long and short fictional forms.

The Injustice Collectors and *The Romantic Egoists*

Auchincloss's early short stories are generally incisive, well-crafted character sketches with crisp, self-expository dialogue. His proclivity, reflected in the titles of his first two collections, is toward conspicuous if less than deviant behavior set against the generally well ordered social background featured in the novels. In a preface to *The Injustice Collectors* Auchincloss attributes his choice of title to the psychiatrist Edmund Bergler, acknowledging that his own use of the term extends well beyond the limits of Bergler's strict medical definition:

I do not purport to use the term in Dr. Bergler's exact medical sense, but in a wider sense to describe people who are looking for injustice, even in a friendly world, because they suffer from a hidden need to feel that the world has wronged them. . . . That a character's undoing or rejection may be the result of his own course of action is hardly surprising, but it may be significant that he has chosen, not only the course but also the result to which it leads.

The characters surveyed in *The Injustice Collectors* are a varied and generally interesting lot. Maud Spreddon, the title character of "Maud," is an early prototype of the intelligent, restless Auchincloss woman; ill at ease in her lawyer father's household, Maud will break her engagement to Halsted Nicholas, her father's partner and a long-time family friend, presumably because she doubts her fitness for marriage. Later, during World War II, she will meet Halsted by chance in London and agree to marry him at last. After Halsted's death in battle two days later, Maud decides to keep their renewed acquaintance a secret from her family: "She did not tell her parents or even Sammy that she had seen Halsted again before his death, or what had passed between them. Such a tale would have made her a worthy object of the pity she had so despised herself for seeking. It was her sorrow, and Halsted would have admired her for facing it alone."

In "The Miracle," which opens the collection, a well-born but self-made tycoon schemes successfully to keep his cherished only son from marrying a somewhat older spinster. "The Fall of a Sparrow" recalls the author's naval service during World War II. "Finish, Good Lady," narrated in the first person by a middle-aged nurse-companion, recalls stresses in the family of one of her elderly patients. "Greg's Peg," told by a prep-school headmaster, revisits the oddly futile life of one Gregory Bakewell, a summer acquaintance, who clung to his indifferent, eccentric mother until his own death in early middle age. On balance, the stories in Auchincloss's first collection are polished and thoughtful, told from a variety of viewpoints; it was not until *The Romantic Egoists* that the author would adumbrate both the form and the style of his later collections, closing the perceived distance between short and long fiction.

Like the "injustice collectors," the "romantic egoists" featured in the second collection differ slightly from the supposed norm. Egoists, not egotists, they tend toward self-absorption, with impossible dreams and ambitions. Perhaps the strongest and most representative tale included in *The Romantic Egoists* is "The Great World and Timothy Colt," in effect a preliminary study toward the novel of the same name in which the title character's obsession is already quite fully developed.

Without exception, the eight stories comprising *The Romantic Egoists* are told by the lawyer Peter Westcott, a semi-autobiographical persona similar to O'Hara's James Malloy. The facts of Westcott's life, however, remain secondary to his observations, and when Westcott functions within the various narratives he is of interest mainly as a foil or inter-locutor. He tells the story of Timmy Colt from the point of view of a younger associate in Timmy's law firm, privy to Timmy's thoughts and decisions; in "Wally," set in Panama during the war, he recalls the amusing, if faintly pathetic efforts of a fellow officer named Walling-ford, a graduate of Cornell University's hotel school, to obtain a transfer to hotel duty. "Billy and the Gargoyles" recalls Westcott's prep-school days, in particular the misadventures of a less adaptable cousin. "The Legends of Henry Everett" contrasts appearance with real-ity in the life and career of the octogenarian senior partner of Westcott's law firm. "The Fortune of Arleus Kane," although it deals with a fa-miliar Auchincloss theme, is perhaps a bit simplistic in its portrayal of a young attorney continually hampered in courtship, career, mar-riage, and politics by the burden of his family's wealth. Nearly one-fourth of the volume, however, is devoted to Auchincloss's original telling of the Timmy Colt story, stopping short of the turnabout and eventual disgrace recorded in the novel. Taken together, the eight stories almost constitute a novel, or a portion of one, except that none of Westcott's diverse acquaintances appear to be acquainted with each other. Significantly, the viewpoint character of Westcott, although sat-isfactory, would never again appear in Auchincloss's fiction, either long or short. His next volume of collected stories, published nearly a de-cade later, would be narrated throughout in the third person, yet would resemble even more closely a novel thanks to the prevalence of shared and recurrent characters.

Powers of Attorney and *The Partners*

Although published just over a decade apart, *Powers of Attorney* and *The Partners* are basically similar in tone, content, and subject matter, as well as in accomplishment, regardless of the fact that the earlier volume was initially marketed as a collection of stories and the second as a novel. Both volumes deal episodically with the problems and personalities of a large, "modern" Wall Street law firm, known as Tower, Tilney, and Webb in *Powers of Attorney,* as Shepard, Putney, and Cox in *The Partners.* In each volume the exposition centers around a responsible, middle-aged partner charged with guiding his colleagues through transitions in the legal profession: Clitus Tilney of Tower, Tilney, and Webb carries the designation of senior partner, while Beekman "Beeky" Ehninger of Shepard, Putney, and Cox holds the somewhat less prestigious title of managing partner. Typically, each firm has at least one eccentric elderly partner, several youngish "drones," and a number of ambitious young associates both with and without Ivy League degrees. Some of the latter are female. To a greater degree than in the novels, Auchincloss's presentation is here tinged with a heavy irony that often approaches broad humor:

Webb stared in fascination at the beautiful, promiscuous, near-naked quarte , with their host of beautiful, near-naked children. Who would have belie d that a scant eighteen months before they had been engaged in no fewer than six bitter lawsuits? And now, with children tumbling over each other and over them (children who hardly knew, perhaps, which adult was a parent and which a step–parent), laughing and sipping gin, making jokes—oh, agony to think of!—of their "little men downtown" who had taken their squabbles with such amusing, passionate seriousness, they might have been the foreground in an advertisement for an exotic foreign car, so congenial, so gay, so pearly-toothed did they all appear. "Rabbits," he muttered angrily to his partner as they turned back to the club house. "They're nothing but rabbits. People like that don't deserve the time the courts waste over them. They should do their breeding without sanction of law!" ("From Bed and Board," *Powers of Attorney*)

In both volumes, Auchincloss's approach to character often recalls the incisive portraits of the seventeenth-century French satirist Jean de la Bruyère, whose work Auchincloss knows well. Unlike the French-

man, however, Auchincloss most frequently manages the delineation
of character through the sustained portrayal of behavior. The spineless
but petulant Rutherford Tower, a partner in Tower, Tilney, and Webb
by sheer force of nepotism, dreams of revenge against his stronger partners and believes that he has found the means when an elegant old
gentleman enlists his help in writing a will; too late, Rutherford will
learn that the old man was a true eccentric, with dozens of worthless
wills scattered across the Eastern seaboard. Morris Madison, another
Tilney partner, deserted by his socialite wife early in his successful
career as a tax specialist, has since devoted all of his spare time to a
diary of social observation inspired by the Duc de Saint-Simon. Some
twenty-five years later Madison will contemplate remarriage to the
widowed Aurelia Starr, carefully selected as "The Single Reader" of the
story's title; by that time, however, Madison's obsession has all but
consumed him, enough so to send the poor woman fleeing for dear life.
Ronny Simmonds, a junior associate in Shepard, Putney, and Cox, has
seen service in Vietnam and is still considering his options when he is
nearly trapped into loveless marriage by the machinations of a female
senior partner and her divorced daughter, possibly a nymphomaniac.
In "The Novelist of Manners," perhaps the most memorable episode
included in *The Partners,* Auchincloss turns his ironic wit not only
upon the law but also upon the writer's craft, with observations as
incisive as any to be found in such nonfiction volumes as *A Writer's
Capital* and *Life, Law and Letters.*

Set in France, "The Novelist of Manners" recounts a clash of wills
between one Dana Clyde, a decidedly "popular" novelist known for his
lurid portrayals of the "jet set," and Leslie Carter, a junior partner who,
as head of the firm's Paris office, has been engaged to defend Clyde
against a libel action from an offended "shyster" lawyer. Young Carter,
an impassioned francophile with some unresolved literary aspirations,
quickly befriends the prosperous middle-aged writer and urges him to
attempt, away from his fast cars and high-living friends, the true literary masterpiece of his career. When the long-awaited volume is at
last ready to appear, with galley proofs mailed to Carter in his capacity
as Clyde's attorney, Carter notes with some surprise that the novel is
little different from the usual Clyde standard, certainly no better; although well aware of Clyde's tendency to use real-life models, especially among lawyers, Carter is nonetheless stung to discover himself
in the character of Gregory Blake, an attorney who marries a glamorous

woman who is his client in a divorce case only to kill himself on the wedding night, having discovered his own impotence. It is Clyde's wife Xenia who will explain to a bewildered Carter both the nature and the extent of his transgressions:

"But is it a great novel? Is it that last great novel of manners of the western world?"

"It is not."

"You say that very positively. Didn't you assure him it would be?"

"I was a fatuous ass. I was Gregory Blake."

"I'm afraid you were worse than that, Leslie. You badgered Dana into writing that book. You never stopped to think it might hurt him. Well, it did. It hurt him terribly. That's why he can't forgive you."

"But I never meant it to hurt him!"

"Of course you didn't. You're not a sadist. But it still did. You see, Dana had a secret fantasy. He liked to think of himself as a genius, but a genius manqué. He liked to tell himself that if it hadn't been for his love of the good life—the *douceur de vivre,* as he always called it—he might have been another Flaubert. "Ah, if only I could work as he worked," he used to say. Well, he worked at Malaga, he really did. And you see what he produced. He sees it, too. He can no longer kid himself that he could ever have written *Madame Bovary.* So he took his revenge."

Apart from its finely honed satire of "life, law and letters," "The Novelist of Manners" is notable also for the implied view of the convention reflected in its title. By implication, the novel of manners has long since been deserted by such "serious" practitioners as Auchincloss and his predecessors, leaving the field to slick, prolific craftsmen like the fictional Dana Clyde. The reading public, denied the talents even of O'Hara and Marquand, is thus increasingly dependent for its knowledge of society upon the commercial product most commonly peddled in supermarkets and at airport newsstands.

Ironically, the mere existence of such volumes as *Powers of Attorney* and *The Partners* suggests a viable direction for future would-be novelists of manners: Combining the incisiveness of the short story, particularly as practiced by O'Hara in his later years, with the unifying vision peculiar to the novel, Auchincloss's hybrid ventures provide rich and satisfying reading, even as their episodic structure might make them suitable fare for such casual readers as the airline passenger. Unfortunately, Auchincloss's experiments in combining two genres have yielded distinctly uneven results, with *Powers of Attorney* and *The Partners* emerging as the most successful such efforts to date.

Tales of Manhattan and *Second Chance*

Between *Powers of Attorney* and *The Partners* Auchincloss further enhanced his reputation as a writer of short fiction with two collections that, although less unified than the two volumes just cited, consist of tales related to one another by common elements of theme and structure. Published soon after the author's most successful novels, both *Tales of Manhattan* (1967), and *Second Chance* (1970) helped sustain Auchincloss's reputation as a keen observer of manners and morals.

Divided into three approximately equal subgroups, each containing closely interrelated pieces, *Tales of Manhattan* contains some of his strongest, most memorable writing, particularly in the fictional memoirs of the auctioneer Roger Jordan. An avid student of human nature with the instincts of a sleuth, Jordan delves beneath the polished surface of the social and artistic world to reveal the darker side of collectors and artists alike: "Stirling's Folly" uncovers, beneath the remnants of a distinguished collection, a long-buried intrigue of self-indulgence, arson, and betrayal; in "The Moon and Six Guineas" Jordan discovers incontrovertible evidence that a group of near-pornographic sketches, thought to represent painter John Howland's licentious senility, are in fact juvenilia portraying the artist's stiff, straitlaced parents in positions of amorous abandon. In "Collector of Innocents" Jordan deals perceptively and, in the end, diplomatically with an aging clubman once committed to canvas as a happy, carefree child. The two remaining Jordan stories, however, reach beyond the art world into territory even more familiar to readers of the author's longer fiction. "The Question of the Existence of Waring Stohl" recalls the world of letters as seen in *Sybil* and *Pursuit of the Prodigal,* while "The Money Juggler" clearly adumbrates the plot, theme, and characters of Auchincloss's subsequent novel, *A World of Profit.*

"The Question of the Existence of Waring Stohl,"among the more incisive and ironic of Auchincloss's short stories, cleverly reverses the perceived roles of predator and victim. At first, it appears even to the perceptive Roger Jordan that the brash literary upstart Waring Stohl is taking unfair advantage of the genteel, dilettantish professor and critic, Nathaniel Streebe. Stohl, however, knows himself to be in precarious health and suggests to an astonished Jordan that the situation is indeed quite the opposite: Streebe is the true opportunist, now pressuring Stohl to write and publish a second novel. Soon after Stohl's early death, Streebe will further enhance his own reputation with an edition of the younger man's unpublished journals, complete with commentary, bearing the same title as the Auchincloss short story.

In "The Money Juggler" Auchincloss presents his basic outline for *A World of Profit,* including such supporting characters as the writer Hilary Knowles and the attorney John Grau. In the shorter version all the male principals are portrayed as members of Jordan's Columbia University graduating class of 1940; the title character, prototypical of Jay Livingston, is here known as Lester Gordon, having traded his original surname of Kinsky for that of some maternal relatives originally known as Ginsberg. Although *A World of Profit* remains, on balance, among the author's weaker novels, it is nonetheless more successful as fiction than "The Money Juggler," in which the limitations of the shorter form force a substitution of crammed narration for the dialogue and action later portrayed in the novel.

The second group of stories, entitled "Arnold and Degener, One Chase Manhattan Plaza," surveys territory similar to that covered in *Powers of Attorney,* later to be revisited in *The Partners;* the main difference, from a technical point of view, is that the characters here speak for themselves, having been asked by the senior partner to contribute to a history of their firm. "The Matrons," comprising the final section, includes Auchincloss's only published play, *The Club Bedroom,* later successfully televised with Ruth White cast in the main role of Mrs. Ruggles.

Second Chance, subtitled *Tales of Two Generations,* combines in most of its component tales the intense irony of *Tales of Manhattan* with a strong sense of society in transition. "The Prince and the Pauper," perhaps the most masterful and memorable of the stories, has been discussed in chapter 5; the title tale, previously unpublished, is notable for its double-edged portrayal of two middle-aged men whose wives happen to be sisters. Gilbert Van Ness, after two decades of subjugation to his wife's large, close-knit family, emerges from psychoanalysis with a fierce determination to start over again, changing both wives and careers. His former brother-in-law, known only as Joe, is alternately fascinated and repelled as he observes—and records—Gilbert's successful if ruthless rise to power. Among the other notable stories in

Second Chance are "The Cathedral Builder," describing the obsession of a miserly nonagenarian lawyer, and "The Sacrifice," in which an aging jurist contemplates the prevalence and consequences of violence. Notable for its polished prose as well as for its varied insights, *Second Chance* compares favorably with such earlier collections as *The Injustice Collectors* and *The Romantic Egoists,* even as it lacks the added "novelistic" dimension found in *Powers of Attorney* and *The Partners.*

The Winthrop Covenant and *The Book Class*

In *The Winthrop Covenant* Auchincloss attempted yet another sort of fusion between long and short fiction with a series of episodes purporting to show the Puritan ethic as formed and deformed from colonial times through the narrative present. Centering more or less upon the archetypal Winthrop family, rich in clergymen, lawyers, and diplomats, the various component stories are decidedly uneven in tone and quality, yielding an overall result considerably less successful than *Powers of Attorney* or *The Partners.* Curiously, however, Auchincloss continued to value *The Winthrop Covenant* among his favorite works and would, during the following decade, develop two of its episodes into full-length novels: *Watchfires* (1982) owes much to the story "In the Beauty of the Lilies Christ Was Born Across the Sea"; similarly, "The Penultimate Puritan" contains, in germ, most of the plot and characters of *Honorable Men* (1985), although the characters have different names. A third episode, "The Mystic Journal," harks back to *The Rector of Justin* in its evocation of a private school for boys during the early years of the twentieth century. The remaining tales, although hardly negligible, do little to enhance the author's already estimable reputation as a master of both long and short fiction.

Although published and presented as a novel, *The Book Class* (1984) remains more closely linked, in theme and structure, to Auchincloss's short stories than to his earlier novels. Like *The Winthrop Covenant,* it represents still another effort to call into question the presumed boundaries between long and short fiction.

More anecdotal than episodic in structure, *The Book Class* represents the efforts of the narrator, Christopher Gates, to understand, and indeed to explain, the often obscure lives of his mother and her friends, founding members of the "book class." The class itself, stopping always short of true education or enlightenment, exemplifies the peculiar paradox that Christopher sees in the women's now-vanished life-style:

Neither feminist nor feminine, the New York society matrons born around 1890 nonetheless exercised considerable power among their families and friends. Their power, however, was often exercised in secret, and it is Christopher's chosen task to afford his readers a peek behind the scenes rendered even more vivid by his singular personal perspective. Having intervened, unsuccessfully, as a youth to prevent his mother's implication in a 1936 financial scandal similar to that described in *The Embezzler,* Chris developed not long thereafter a true vocation for meddling; throughout the action recalled, the narrator himself often figures as participant as well as observer.

Cast in the form of a memoir, *The Book Class* lacks the structure normally expected of the novel and is nearly devoid of plot. Following the drift of his own memories and argument, Chris moves from one member of the book class to another, even back again, pausing to ruminate on such questions as viewpoint and narrative voice: In the case of Justine Bannard, for example, Chris Gates can only speculate on how Justine must have contrived to keep her marriage intact after learning from young Chris that it was threatened. Published by itself, as a self-contained unit, the Justine Bannard chapter would be a typical, even distinguished Auchincloss short story; so also would Christopher's recollections of Georgia Bristed, whose activities helped to convict one of his former classmates for treason. Unfortunately, such episodes—or anecdotes—remain trapped within the apparent framework of a novel, which demands that they be read consecutively, and together. On balance, however, *The Book Class* is in all likelihood a more successful effort than *The Winthrop Convenant,* despite—or perhaps due to—its less ambitious scope.

Narcissa and Other Fables

Just as he continued, throughout the 1970s and well into the 1980s, to write conventionally plotted novels, so also did Auchincloss continue to write conventional short stories. *Narcissa and Other Fables,* published during 1983, is a conventional story collection, including some items initially appearing elsewhere and others published for the first time. If there is a common element among the stories it is the author's keen sense of irony, here honed and polished to a fine satirical edge. In "Charade" the well-derived but impoverished bluestocking Madge Dyett, retrieved from Auchincloss's long-discarded first novelistic effort, engages in delicate "mind-games" with a rich couple seeking a wife for their blatantly homosexual son, a most reluctant law student; in "Equitable Awards," discussed in an earlier chapter, a would-be divorcée in early middle age finds herself caught between the expectations of two generations without having truly belonged to either. There is, to be sure, a fabulistic cast to many of the tales, as to much good short fiction, but the designation "fable" applies most specifically to the very short fictions appearing at the end of the volume as "Sketches of the Nineteen Seventies," originally published in *New York* magazine as "Stories of Death and Society." Never more than one and one-half pages in length, the fabulistic "Sketches" most resemble rather grim jokes, easily retold, well summarized in the representative titles "Sic transit" and "Do You Know This Man?" In the former the octogenarian heiress of several generations of bankers, invited out of respect, strolls unrecognized through a gathering of young executives, the original bank having since undergone several mergers; the woman is deferred to by reason of her regal bearing, although no one present seems to know who she is. In the latter "fable" an aspirant benefactor seeks immortality through his art collection, only to have his will so construed that he is soon forgotten.

Other notable stories in the collection include the title tale, in which a rich dilettante is expected to pay for her strange compulsion to pose in the nude, and "Marley's Chain," set in Virginia, in which a retired bachelor diplomat reconsiders the option of marriage. Perhaps typically those stories, like "Charade" and many anecdotes in *The Book Class,* are set during the 1930s, the period of the author's richest recollections. Less typical, and somewhat less successful, is "The Cup of Coffee," a broad farce dealing with office politics in a contemporary setting; although humorous, the story is hampered by the flatness and implausibility of the principal characters. "The Seagull," couched in epistolary form, presents the nearly implausible apologia of an Episcopal priest who has conceived the scope of his "ministry" to include adultery. On balance, however, the collection ranks in style and quality with such earlier efforts as *The Injustice Collectors* and *Tales of Manhattan,* showing that the author has not lost his singular talent for deft exposition in the shorter form.

Taken together, Auchincloss's collected short fictions compose a not inconsiderable body of work. As social observation, they are perhaps as remarkable as those of O'Hara, although fewer in number and somewhat narrower in scope. As an ironist in the short story form, Auchincloss is perhaps outshone only by John Updike, whose frequent experiments with form, style, and voice are even bolder, with frequently remarkable effect. Auchincloss's principal contribution, however, appears to be in his frequent pressure against the boundaries that appear to separate the short story from the novel; perhaps future prose writers would do well to follow his example.

Chapter Seven
Essays and Criticism

With *Reflections of a Jacobite,* first published in book form during 1961, Auchincloss began to distinguish himself also as a perceptive essayist and critic, covering a wide range of literary and historical subjects in the same lucid prose style that marks his published fiction. Having heeded his former professor's advice *not* to pursue a doctorate in English literature, Auchincloss the critic has remained well clear of the academic establishment with its changing schools and fashions; his approach, throughout ten volumes of expository prose published between 1961 and 1984, is resolutely that of the erudite, cultivated "amateur" writing in depth upon subjects that have managed to attract and hold his interest. Typically, his articles are short and incisive, suitable in form and style to the periodicals in which some of them first appeared; less typical, and fewer in number, are books and monographs dealing with a single theme or subject, such as *Pioneers and Caretakers* (1965), concerning with American women novelists, *Reading Henry James* (1975), or *False Dawn* (1984), a psychological group portrait of European noblewomen in the seventeenth century. Other volumes, such as *Richelieu* (1973) and *Persons of Consequence: Queen Victoria and her Circle* (1977), consist largely of illustrations bound together with the author's lucid commentary.

In title, form, and subject matter *Reflections of a Jacobite* neatly sets out the course, and the range, of the nonfiction writings that would follow over the two subsequent decades. The author, an avowed and unrepentant disciple of Henry James, brings that perspective to bear upon such apparently disparate subjects as Thackeray, Louis XIV, John O'Hara, and the diarist George Templeton Strong, whose life and career would later inspire the novel *Watchfires.* James himself is of course a frequent subject, as are such British forebears as George Meredith and Anthony Trollope. Perhaps the strongest of the essays, "Proust's Picture of Society," goes well beyond received notions about Proust to anticipate two decades of subsequent Proust scholarship. Significantly Proust, like James, would remain a favorite and frequent essay subject for Auchincloss, accounting for some of his strongest expository writing.

Arguably, given the fact of his "amateur" status as a critic, Auchincloss might never have found a forum or audience for his essays had he not first established himself as a novelist; even such publications as the *Nation* and *Partisan Review* (in which portions of *Reflections of a Jacobite* first appeared) do not, as a matter of course, rush to publish submissions from Wall Street lawyers, no matter how well-read they might be. It was thus his reputation as a novelist, however modest in the early 1960s, that secured Auchincloss a ready audience for his essays, as well as university press contracts for *Pioneers and Caretakers, Edith Wharton,* and, indeed, his autobiographical volume *A Writer's Capital.* Since *Reflections of a Jacobite,* moreover, Auchincloss has been in frequent demand as the author of book reviews and other occasional pieces, several of which are reprinted in *Life, Law and Letters* (1979).

As perhaps befits the work of an "extramural" critic, Auchincloss's expository essays range from the casual and anecdotal to the profound, with little external distinction between modes; what is more, he does not, as a more formally trained critic would feel bound to do, attempt to exhaust a particular subject or, except on occasion, to explore its historical background: *Reading Henry James,* for example, makes no claim to completeness; in it, Auchincloss depends upon the biographical research of Leon Edel and acknowledges, in addition, the current "industry" of James scholarship, all the while offering an extremely personal and independent view. In *Life, Law and Letters* Auchincloss records in passing his recent, unsuccessful efforts to obtain publishers' rights for a cut version of Proust's *A la Recherche du temps perdu,* an attempt that he justifies as follows:

I belong to the unfashionable but unrepentant persuasion that finds the Albertine passages a serious flaw in *A la Recherche du Temps Perdu.* The last time I read through the seven novels I did so in inverse order. It confirmed something that I have long suspected, namely, that the narrator's affair with Albertine acts as a drag as the work progresses. Reading the story backward I found my interest, on the contrary, increasing in intensity until *Du Côté de Chez Swann* provided a fitting and tremendous climax. Only in the last third of *A l'Ombre des Jeunes Filles en Fleurs,* where the narrator meets Albertine and her girl friends on the beach at Balbec, did I find the process reversed.[1]

As much the professional novelist as he is the amateur critic, Auchincloss apparently sees no harm to be done in emending (thus

amending) Proust's magnum opus to render *A la Recherche* more plea-
surable to the reader approaching Proust for the first time, forwards or
backwards. As in his creative work, Auchincloss the critic remains
firmly committed to the pleasure principle, thus anticipating (and, in
a way, transcending) many of the banalities that have been discovered
by much recent, "post-structuralist" criticism. Of course, the academic
establishment, such as it still stands, would never tolerate the cutting
of a major work to bring it into conformity with such personal, arbitrary standards (notwithstanding Anthony Burgess's 1968 version of *A
Shorter Finnegans Wake*, a venture more newsworthy than useful even at
the time). Throughout his essays, however, Auchincloss retains (as
here) the clear voice of common sense, tinged as it may be with the
accents of intellectual snobbery. The reader (of Auchincloss or of
Proust) might well take exception to the amateur critic's vaunted familiarity with a work that few nonspecialists have found time to read
more than once, let alone backwards. Here as elsewhere, though, Auchincloss makes a strong appeal to common sense, linking the appre-
ciation of literary art with the enjoyment that it must produce in order
to be worthy of attention in the first place.

Reading Henry James, consisting in part of essays originally published
elsewhere, further exemplifies the author's approach to "practical" criticism underlain by common sense. Taking exception to Edel's assertion
that James derived much of the dramatic, "scenario" effect of his mature fiction from his experiments as a playwright, Auchincloss argues
persuasively that the "scenario" effect is nowhere less in evidence than
in James's plays, pedestrian at best. Indeed, he claims, James's sense
of the dramatic is strongest in fictional narration where no dialogue is
present:

What James never learned was how to make his characters reveal themselves
in dialogue. They all talk alike, and artificially. This makes no difference in
the novels. There the characters are so vividly presented in the prose that we
are delighted to have them speak beautifully—as if they were declaiming
poetry or singing. Stylization of dialogue occurs in many of our greatest works
of fiction. But when the curtain rises on a drawing room of our own day, the
actors have only the vernacular in which to introduce and describe themselves.
James never addressed himself to this problem. I doubt that he even recognized it. What he really wanted was to be a playwright, rather than to write
plays—a common failing in novelists.[2]

Concerning *The Ambassadors,* Auchincloss readily admits that his view of Lambert Strether changed and evolved as he himself approached the character's age of fifty-five:

> Yet the years have taught me how desperately human beings, particularly in later life, can try to fool themselves. Strether has fallen in love with Paris and with the love that exists between Chad and Madame de Vionnet. He has never felt such exaltation before, and it is necessary for him to put it on some kind of a basis that he can understand. There is in him a stubborn, transcendental idealism that, if quixotic, is still finer than the coarser idealism of Mrs. Newsome. For all the latter's high-mindedness, she is quick to assume that Madame de Vionnet is not even the apology for a decent woman. Strether wears his New England conscience with a difference. Where Mrs. Newsome tends to condemn, he tends to extenuate. Because he sees Chad made over by a wonderfully civilized woman, he must reject the idea that they could have the kind of liaison that he has always associated with less wonderful changes in young men. To put things in his own special kind of high order he must adopt the premise that the attachment is virtuous.[3]

Resolutely "extramural" and discursive, even idiosyncratic on occasion, Auchincloss's particular approach to criticism nonetheless brings the reader closer to the work under discussion through the disclosure of *one* reader's intense interaction. Nor is Auchincloss's attention confined to such major canonical figures as Proust, James, or even Wharton: "Is George Eliot Salvageable?" poses a pertinent question in one of Auchincloss's earlier essays, a question to be answered in the qualified negative after a thoughtful, well-informed consideration of the woman novelist's major works. Other authors treated with equal attention to detail in Auchincloss's various essays include Paul Bourget, George Meredith, Anthony Trollope, and Theodore Dreiser, whose energy and enthusiasm are seen as transcending the limits of his rather pedestrian style. Literature, however, is not the only frequent subject of Auchincloss the essayist: *False Dawn,* published during 1984, brings to fruition an interest in seventeenth-century France already expressed in shorter pieces scattered throughout *Reflections of a Jacobite* and *Life, Law and Letters.* Literary figures, although treated in considerable depth, are by no means the exclusive subject of the author's exposition; as a practicing attorney, Auchincloss remains particularly sensitive to persons and questions of diplomacy and politics, offering a view of history that is at once highly personal and extremely well informed.

As early as *Reflections of a Jacobite,* Auchincloss expressed a close familiarity with the memoirs of the Duc de Saint-Simon, a work of social observation that continues to fascinate and interest him. Versailles itself, with its stratifications and incessant intrigue, of course figures prominently in the history of the novel of manners, with repercussions in the fiction of Proust and in that of Auchincloss himself. "I shall keep reverting to the analogy of the school," observes Auchincloss in his early piece on Saint-Simon, "because it seems to me the key to the puzzle of Versailles. It was a school, except there were no diplomas. Louis XIV did not allow anyone to graduate." "Saint-Simon," he goes on,

is the perfect guide to the era because his philosophy is almost a parody of the prevailing philosophy. He believed that all history could be boiled down to the simple question of precedence. A good man was one who knew his rung on the ladder and remained perched on it. A great man was one who saw to it that everyone else remained perched on theirs. A bad man was one who tried to climb to a higher rung, and a weak man was one who allowed a bad man to climb over him. Any movement on the ladder, up or down, tended to shake the civilized order. At times Saint-Simon carries it so far that he seems more of a caricaturist than a historian. All of France, all of Europe, is lit up against the ludicrous backdrop of the social order.[4]

In *False Dawn,* an older Auchincloss would focus his attention upon the prominent women of the Versailles era, showing their involvement—and influence—in the intrigues that Saint-Simon describes. Invariably noble or royal by birth and/or marriage, the women profiled are less exclusively French, drawn toward Versailles from all over Europe. The author's conclusion, implicit in his choice of title, is that the peculiar, "private-school" atmosphere of Versailles allowed its wellborn, well-read female inhabitants a degree of freedom and assertion that would subsequently fall from fashion, not to reappear until nearly two centuries later. Part history, part speculative essay, *False Dawn* is perhaps best described as an exercise in popular historiography, frequently as engaging to read as it is difficult to classify.

Surveying the Europe that Louis XIV sought to dominate through sheer force of will, Auchincloss more than once sees life imitating art. Of the king's cousin Anne-Marie-Louise d'Orleans, "La grande Mademoiselle," he writes,

It has been said that Mademoiselle was a caricature of a Corneille heroine. But why a caricature? It seems to me that she was a Corneille heroine to the life. People who know the poet only in his greatest tragedies, *Le Cid, Horace* and *Polyeucte,* are not aware how odd he could be in his lesser ones. His women in the latter, like Mademoiselle, are always intoxicated with their exalted rank. They assign the highest dignity to what is apt to strike us as the crassest kind of ambition, and they snipe at each other with a shrillness that Voltaire found unworthy of tragic drama.[5]

In such disparate characters as Mary of Modena, Lady Masham, Queen Anne, Madame de Sévigné, and Mère Angelique of the Jansenist Port-Royal convent, Auchincloss discerns a particular, albeit Cornelian assertiveness that appears to have developed in reaction to the masculine repressiveness practiced by the Sun King. Such, indeed, has not been the prevailing view, and Auchincloss takes considerable pains to establish that century, and not the next one, as the true origin of feminine consciousness:

The death of Louis XIV in 1715 provided a delayed opening of the eighteenth century. It has often been claimed that women dominated the so-called Age of Reason, and in some ways they did, but I suspect that they did not do so to their own ultimate advantage. I suggest that what women really accomplished in the eighteenth century was to harness their force and genius to the chariot of charm, and in so doing to decorate the age with a grace that no age before or since has been able to boast. But what was it, in fact, but decoration? The eighteenth century may have been a women's century, but it was also the century of Boucher and Fragonard.[6]

As befits the author of *A Law for the Lion* and *Portrait in Brownstone,* not to mention *The Book Class,* Auchincloss has approached the subject of *False Dawn* with a keen sense of the real and the imaginary with regard to the power of women. Arguably, the characters profiled in *False Dawn did* exercise more real power then their immediate successors, even though they themselves may have remained unaware of it. Ultimately, however, Auchincloss's exposition ends in a paradox similar to that presented in *The Book Class,* published the same year. In seventeenth-century Europe, as in the Manhattan of the 1930s, the exercise of power by women remained largely covert, unheralded, and frequently unrecognized, hence hard to qualify as "liberation" by the standards of a later time.

Carefully researched, thoughtfully presented, *False Dawn* exemplifies both the strengths and the potential weaknesses of Auchincloss as essayist and critic. Focusing broad erudition upon a relatively narrow subject, he nonetheless finds it advisable, or even necessary, to retell much of modern European history in order to place his chosen subjects against their proper background. As it stands, the volume is a peculiar mixture of the original and the long familiar, belonging (like the illustrated books on Richelieu and the Victorians) more to the loose classification of belles lettres than to either history or criticism. Perhaps too specialized for the general reader, surely too generalized for the specialist, *False Dawn* raises questions of audience. To whom is such a book addressed, and how indeed is it to be classified? To a certain degree, the same questions might be raised concerning *Reading Henry James* as well. On the other hand, the insights contained in both volumes, as elsewhere in Auchincloss's nonfiction, amply repay the potential reader's time and effort. As in his novels and short stories, Auchincloss endeavors in his expository writing both to express and to share the true benefits of a broad cultural background, approaching frequently "hallowed" subjects with a generalist's refreshing common sense.

Chapter Eight
Reflection and Restatement: The Novels after 1970

If there's one thing I know how to parse, it's the mind of an arriviste. They always make the mistake of assuming that society has standards. They can never get it into their heads that we make rules only to break them. Mr. Stiles, for example, assumes that my daughter-in-law, Amy—because she comes from a rather shabby branch of the Chadbourne family and because of that sordid episode with Herman Fidler—must be somehow déclassé. He can't take in that we only hold a woman's past against her when we dislike her anyway.

—Iris Coates to Fanny Lane,
The Country Cousin, 1978

With *The Embezzler,* Auchincloss completed his basic fictional statement, the novelistic canon by which his work is most likely to be judged and remembered. His subsequent novel, *A World of Profit* (1968), developed from one of the *Tales of Manhattan* (1967), announced a third phase of his career as a novelist, characterized by competent, readable, even typical Auchincloss fiction that, however, does little to strengthen or to elucidate the statement already made. The three notable exceptions, *I Come as a Thief* (1972), *The House of the Prophet* (1980), and *Watchfires* (1982) have been discussed at some length in an earlier chapter, insofar as they contribute to the canon; *The Partners* (1974), *The Winthrop Covenant* (1976), and *The Book Class* (1984) have been treated in connection with the author's short fiction. Two additional titles, *The Cat and the King* (1981) and *Exit Lady Masham* (1983), are historical exercises less closely related to Auchincloss's novelistic canon than to his nonfiction volume *False Dawn* (1984) with which they share characters and subject matter. The remaining volumes, like *A World of Profit,* tend to feature characters that are somehow less engaging, rather less plausible than those featured in the novels of the 1950s and 1960s, even as the territory surveyed remains pretty much the same, centering upon the 1930s. They remain, however, both entertaining and informative, notable for the author's keen observation and incise prose.

The Dark Lady and *The Country Cousin*

Published just a year apart, in 1977 and 1978 respectively, *The Dark Lady* and *The Country Cousin* describe intrigues of love and betrayal against the changing background of New York society during the Depression. In both novels, as in *The Embezzler,* the privileged central characters express great concern with what is going on in the nation's capital under Franklin Roosevelt, vaguely sensing also that their lives are about to be changed by recent political events in Europe. The true dramatic tension, however, obtains within and among the characters themselves, influenced only tangentially by the shifting currents of history.

A major structural weakness in both novels, it would seem, is the significant role afforded in each to a truly meddlesome, even villainous character whose motivations, although "explained," tend nonetheless to strain the reader's credulity. Most of the plot of *The Dark Lady,* indeed, springs from the possibly deranged machinations of the self-made magazine journalist Ivy Trask; in *The Country Cousin,* meanwhile, the mere fact that lawyer Fred Stiles is an arriviste does little to explain the destructive force of his resentment. In the presence of such flattened villains, the action of both novels frequently veers off toward melodrama, detracting from the balance that obtains in such earlier novels as *Portrait in Brownstone* or *The Embezzler,* where the characters and their motivations are somewhat more evenly matched.

In *The Dark Lady,* as earlier in *Pursuit of the Prodigal,* Auchincloss credibly evokes the strange, hybrid world of fashion journalism, inhabited by fiercely independent women and gossipy male homosexuals. Ivy Trask, born around 1880 and orphaned at an early age, has by her mid-fifties risen to a position of considerable power and influence on the editorial staff of *Tone* magazine when she acquires as her protégée one Elesina Dart, the title character, a twice-divorced former stage actress in her early thirties with a fondness for strong drink. Ivy, consigned to spinsterhood by her tart tongue and diminutive stature, is quick to spot Elesina's abiding "star" quality, little diminished by the recent reverses in her life. Elesina, well-derived and socially acceptable despite her stage career, appears to Ivy as the greatest potential success of Ivy's life; on the pretext that a magazine career will provide precisely the second chance that Elesina needs, Ivy proceeds to "push" the younger woman both professionally and socially, even scheming to break up the marriage of two old friends in order to provide Elesina with a suitable third husband. Judge Irving Stein, married for some thirty years to the former Clara Clarkson, will yield to Ivy's machinations and, in time, install Elesina as chatelaine of his art-filled "country place" in Westchester. When the judge's health begins to fail not long thereafter, Ivy will scheme to push Elesina into an affair with David Stein, the judge's youngest son, who has sided with his mother, remaining opposed to his father's divorce and remarriage. Once again, Ivy will prevail; Elesina, for the first time in her life, fancies herself truly in love. When the judge dies, however, she refuses David's proposal of marriage, a proposal based on his condition that they both renounce any claim to his father's vast estate. Ever the idealist, David enlists in the British army early in 1940 and is killed in action at Dunkirk. A brief final section recounts Elesina's postwar political career, also stage-managed by Ivy, whose slanderous campaign tactics will cause a definitive rupture with Elesina after the latter's election to Congress. Ivy, by then in her seventies, impulsively jumps out a window to her death; the action of the novel does not long survive her, although Elesina's political successes probably will.

Although long fascinated, as shown in *Portrait in Brownstone, False Dawn,* and *The Book Class,* with the covert exercise of power by women, Auchincloss has somehow failed to create in Ivy Trask a truly credible character; by association, his portrait of Elesina tends to suffer as well. Although vain and artificial in the accepted manner of stage people, Elesina still comes across as too strong a character, in her own right, to be so consistently manipulated by someone like Ivy Trask, whose motivations remain obscure except possibly to herself. The novel, however, is not without its definite merits; as elsewhere, Auchincloss achieves a superior social portrait of the 1930s, and even of the early 1950s; similarly, the dinner-party conversations at the Steins contain some highly entertaining speculation about Shakespeare, both the plays and the sonnets, thanks to Elesina's appearance as the "Dark Lady" in a play based on the sonnets. More than once, the reader is reminded of Auchincloss's critical volume, *Motiveless Malignity,* (1969) dealing with Shakespeare in depth. It is possible, moreover, that the author might well have imagined Ivy Trask as a figure of "motiveless malignity." Unfortunately, such a character is more easily realized on the stage than in the novel, where greater dimension is needed.

A similarly "motiveless malignity" tends to mar *The Country Cousin*, a generally stronger novel that otherwise compares favorably with such earlier efforts as *The Great World and Timothy Colt* or *Pursuit of the Prodigal*. Like those two novels, *The Country Cousin* is concerned primarily with a successful lawyer's inner trials of conscience; unlike Timmy Colt, however, James Coates will risk disbarment to protect the woman he loves, not to repudiate her. It is Fred Stiles, Jamey's slightly younger law partner, whose vindictive resentment of Jamey tends to strike a false note. Fred, although a distinctly minor character, demands more than his share of attention in the novel by reason of his sheer nastiness.

At best a "poor relation" to some old New York families, reared in New Jersey by his druggist's-daughter mother, Fred Stiles has nonetheless managed, by husbanding his family's limited resources, to attend both private school and Yale, including the latter's law school, rising to partnership in a major Wall Street firm before the age of thirty. Notwithstanding, he has carried throughout his thirty-six years an almost incredible burden of resentment, heightened by invited snubs during his college years and now focused almost entirely upon his firm's managing partner, Jamey Coates. By the time of the novel Jamey's mere existence has become a permanent affront to Fred; in the world as Fred sees it, a man like Jamey—small in stature, unprepossessing in looks, descended from a founder of the firm—should be a nonentity, a cipher. Instead, Jamey Coates is a superior, highly professional practitioner of the law, eminently capable of guiding the firm through periods of progress and transition. Jamey, for his part, holds no animus toward Fred and is quite unaware of the other's resentment until the action reaches a climax, as Jamey begins to suspect his partner of sharp practice. Fred, in fact, would like nothing better than to destroy Jamey, having already raped Jamey's pregnant wife in a spirit of unconcealed blackmail. As with Ivy Trask, the destructive impulse appears hardly justified, even assuming the background information supplied by the author. Before such a sworn enemy as Fred, Jamey's inner conflict—between the letter and the spirit of the law, as seen through the eyes of love—is somehow diminished, even trivialized, and the novel loses much of its potential impact.

Although Jamey Coates stands squarely at the center of the novel, it is his future wife, Amy Hunt, the "country cousin" of the title, to whom the reader is first introduced. Unassuming, even mousy in appearance, Amy nonetheless feels and exudes a strong sensuality to which few men are immune. The orphaned daughter of a Connecticut Episcopal priest, Amy has come to New York as a paid companion of Miss Dolly Chadbourne, an immensely rich elderly cousin. Jamey Coates, as Miss Chadbourne's attorney, frequently visits her apartment and is about to declare his feelings for Amy when the latter suddenly elopes with Dolly's nephew Herman Fidler, who in his early thirties has grown tired of both his wife and his job. Herman has worked, without enthusiasm or advancement, for a brokerage house, supported principally by the unearned income of his extravagant and shrewish wife Naomi. Amy Hunt, a spiritual relative of such earlier Auchincloss females as Sybil Hilliard and Eloise Dilworth, has suddenly awakened in Herman a long-dormant desire to resign from his job and try his hand at painting. Together but unmarried, Amy and Herman move into a Greenwich Village garret; it is there that Jamey Coates, as attorney and would-be mediator, finds Amy and persuades her to return to Miss Chadbourne. On his way out he impulsively declares his own feelings; although Amy does not respond, she can at least be sure of Jamey's support over the months to follow. Herman Fidler, meanwhile, adamantly refuses to return to Naomi and their daughters, even if he must live in the garret alone. The central crisis of the novel derives from Dolly Chadbourne's determination to disinherit her nephew and divert his share to his "abandoned" daughters; even after Amy has deserted Herman and returned to her old job, thus fulfilling her part of Dolly's stipulation, Dolly will delay destroying the codicil leaving Herman's share to the two small girls. Soon thereafter, Dolly suffers a stroke and begins losing her mind; when she dies of a subsequent stroke, with the codicil still intact, Amy will tear up the document herself, leaving an all-too-willing and loving Jamey with the responsibility of suppressing the evidence. Their relationship, soon leading to marriage, thus develops under a cloud, with neither partner giving much thought to the fact that Fred Stiles witnessed Dolly's signature on the codicil. Herman Fidler, meanwhile, succeeds so well as an artist that he is soon in a position to restore the funds diverted to his use by Amy's impulsive act.

Naomi Fidler's subsequent remarriage to the "eligible bachelor" Fred Stiles, a contrivance that further strains the reader's credulity, will soon bring matters to a head. Fred, claiming interest in the matter on behalf of his newly acquired stepdaughters, refreshes his memory of the Chadbourne estate and confronts Amy with his deductions, thus frightening her into sexual submission. Jamey, meanwhile, has begun to suspect Fred, in quite another matter, of conspiring to bribe a judge. Like Timmy Colt, Jamey is such a purist that he proves quite willing to face disbarment himself as the price of discrediting Fred Stiles. Herman Fidler, however, intervenes to "save" the situation by restoring his daughters' legacy, on condition that Jamey drop his charges against Fred; for good or for ill, he argues, Fred is the stepfather of his children, who might suffer from his disbarment. Reluctantly, Jamey agrees to Herman's terms, thus placing neither Fred's career nor his own in jeopardy. The novel thus ends on an uneasy note of compromise: Jamey's marriage and career will remain intact, but not without a permanent tarnish of disillusionment.

Reminiscent, in its finest moments, of both *Pursuit of the Prodigal* and *The Embezzler, The Country Cousin* yet falls somewhat short of either novel in maintaining the reader's interest. The major plot device, that of Dolly Chadbourne's will, is perhaps too intricate to be fully workable; Amy's story, meanwhile, tends to intrude upon that of her husband. Jamey Coates, thanks in part to the raw villainy of his antagonist Fred Stiles, seems at times too "good" to be true, giving the reader an uneasy impression that Fred Stiles may be right. In Reese Parmelee, even in Tony Lowder of *I Come as a Thief,* there is more than a hint of recklessness that makes the character believable; Jamey Coates, by contrast, is just a bit of a bore, as drab and unexceptionable as his wife's outward appearance. On balance, however, *The Country Cousin* emerges as a stronger and more entertaining novel than *The Dark Lady,* with a number of memorable passages.

Honorable Men and *Diary of a Yuppie*

Perhaps predictably, the interlocking themes of privilege, responsibility, and power continued to dominate Auchincloss's published fiction well into the 1980s, in such volumes as *Honorable Men* (1985) and *Diary of a Yuppie* (1986). Like Jamey Coates and countless others before him, the author's featured male characters would continue to struggle with their consciences in public and in private, sometimes stretching principle to fit reality.

Honorable Men, developed from the final episode in *The Winthrop Covenant,* profiles the life and career of a dedicated public servant who finally, probably too late, comes to question his government's involvement in Vietnam. Told in part from the viewpoint of Alida Struthers Benedict, the protagonist's estranged wife, *Honorable Men* dwells perhaps too much on the past at the expense of the narrative present; on the pretext of exploring Chip Benedict's background in an attempt to "explain" his development, Auchincloss again revisits the 1930s, with vivid scenes recalling the prewar "country life" at the University of Virginia law school; unlike the author, however, Chip Benedict is married by the time he enrolls.

Like Jamey Coates, Timmy Colt, and Reese Parmelee, Chip Benedict is a man of high, even inflexible principle and, as such, a tempting target for those who would bring him down. Chip's lifelong antagonist, Chester "Chessy" Bogart, is a somewhat better realized version of Fred Stiles; like Fred, Chessy is a social climber and a cynic who will ultimately express his contempt by seducing the wife of the highminded protagonist. Chessy's resentment, however, is more easily understood than Fred's, deriving mainly from a plagiarism incident at Virginia in which Chip's rectitude obliged his classmate (until then, his friend) to change law schools.

Somewhat to the novel's detriment, the ultimate confrontation between Chessy and Chip occurs not on a matter of principle concerning foreign policy, but over the rather more mundane matter of divorce, in which Alida chooses Bogart as her advocate. Against the backdrop of the war in Vietnam, an event that has already estranged Chip from his grown children, Chip will then attempt to create for himself a new life with Violet Crane, who has served as his secretary in Washington. As in "The Penultimate Puritan," the short story from which the novel grew, the protagonist's crisis of conscience derives less from matters of principle than from what might be termed the "mid-life crisis." In the case of Dexter Fairchild, engaged in a torrid affair with his sister-in-law while his wife consorts with abolitionists, the interaction of personal and political concerns is so deftly managed as to appear quite plausible; here, however, Chip Benedict's failing marriage tends to dominate the foreground to the detriment of the political situation described. So too does Chip's problematical acquaintance with Chessy Bogart, who sees both himself and Alida as victims of Chip's lust for power. Chessy, of course, sees only the negative side of his former friend and hero, yet his criticisms are not easily dismissed; as described and revealed, Chip Benedict *does* tend to slight persons in favor of principles, remaining willfully deaf—until midway through the war in Vietnam—to opinions different from his own. Unfortunately, despite the complexity of the characters and the evident affinities with earlier Auchincloss novels, *Honorable Men* never quite transcends the limitations of the short story from which it evolved. Length alone does not a novel make, and except for the character of Chessy there is little depth or detail to be gained in the transformation from "The Penultimate Puritan" to *Honorable Men*. The main female character, Alida in the novel, is still a borderline alcoholic, having failed either to make the marriage work or to develop her own potential as a person; as in the short story, she agrees to grant her husband his freedom, turning to her son, a draft dodger and possibly a homosexual. Alida's narration closes the novel as follows:

I went to my desk and scribbled out a desperate cable to Dana. I told him that I had agreed to a divorce and that his father was planning to remarry. I begged him not to object if I were to fly over to Stockholm and stay in a hotel in his neighborhood. I promised not to interfere with his life there. I ended with the words "Darling, I need you. Please!" But I wondered whether, in the sternness of his dedication to a cause of which I had been at best a wobbly support, he would see fit to stretch out a hand. It would be just my luck to see puritanism take its last twisted stand in both my children.

Had Auchincloss departed further from the data already recorded in "The Penultimate Puritan," he might well have fashioned, out of the Vietnam crisis, a novel as compelling as *Watchfires* or *The Embezzler*, with Chessy Bogart and Chip Benedict squared off against each other in the manner of Rex Geer and Guy Prime; as it stands, however, *Honorable Men* falls considerably short of the two earlier novels in perceived documentary authority as in dramatic impact. Arguably, the Vietnam experience was still too recent to afford the historical perspective obtained even in *The Embezzler*.

Thanks in part to the author's topical choice of title (from which his editors sought to dissuade him), *Diary of a Yuppie* would prove to be one of Auchincloss's greater popular successes, leading to his first sale of film-option rights since *The Rector of Justin*. Profiting, to some degree at least, from the lukewarm reception of *Honorable Men*, Auchincloss in his subsequent novel moved his main focus to the narrative present, adapting his perennial concerns to embrace a later generation of lawyers. In a sense Robert Service is a latter-day Timothy Colt, even as his name recalls that of the duty-bound Dexter Fairchild. Service, it seems, is the son of a lawyer who chose to remain with his firm as a permanent associate after being passed over for partnership; young Robert, succeeding his father in the law, determines to avenge his failure by taking the profession by storm. Thus driven, Robert, like Timmy, will rise quickly toward the top, amid frequent crises both professional and personal; also like Timmy, he will return to his wife after a shattering extramarital infatuation. Although he shares Chip Benedict's disregard for the human element, Robert is on balance a somewhat more dimensional and "sympathetic" character than Chip; as narrator, allowed to speak for himself, he is at least capable of viewing his own actions with irony and some measure of detachment. *Diary of a Yuppie,* published just as Auchincloss entered his seventieth year, thus shows the author in full vigor, with more novels and nonfiction planned to follow his retirement from legal practice at the end of 1986.

Chapter Nine
Conclusions: Limitations and Achievement

No doubt, one major obstacle to the reception and assessment of Auchincloss's work has been its daunting, steadily increasing volume, with at least one new book of fiction or nonfiction published yearly; as the author contemplates retirement from his law firm, with more free time to complete his various writing projects, his annual output is likely to increase, rendering even more difficult the task of the critic who would evaluate and classify his unquestionable contribution to world literature.

Fifty years hence, Auchincloss's characteristic choice of locale and subject matter may no longer be perceived as limiting—not, at least, with regard to the major novels of the 1960s. Indeed, it already appears shortsighted of Auchincloss's immediate contemporaries not to have seen in his New York, and his New Yorkers, a microcosm of American politics and power. In time, readers returning to Auchincloss's novels should also be able to perceive, beneath their polished surface, a current of moral, ethical, and even religious concern that is rare in the work of a Protestant writer. *Watchfires,* to take one example among many, goes straight to the center of responsibility as it relates to power, showing the human frailty beneath the seemingly monolithic institutions of government and law. A future critic, indeed, might profitably explore the affinities among Auchincloss and such Roman Catholic novelists as François Mauriac, Graham Greene, Wilfrid Sheed, and Piers Paul Read.

Unfortunately, the sheer quantity of Auchincloss's fiction has tended to obscure its quality. Although Auchincloss, unlike Mauriac or Ernest Hemingway, appears quite capable of distinguishing treasure from trash in his work, and has been known to destroy completed manuscripts that failed to suit him, he has nonetheless remained sufficiently prolific to attenuate the long-range impact of his strongest literary achievements. At times, he indeed appears to be damaging his own case through repetition, with paler imitations of his earlier work or with novels expanded from short stories previously published. The latter practice, although eminently successful in the case of *Watchfires* or *The Great World and Timothy Colt,* tends to work to the author's disadvantage in such frankly lesser efforts as *A World of Profit* and *Honorable Men.* The current increase in critical interest concerning Auchincloss's work suggests, however, the possibility of significant interaction between the author and his commentators—a process long and inexplicably delayed—allowing him, in the leisure of retirement, to meet and even to surpass the standard of his earlier fiction.

Paradoxically, had Auchincloss written nothing after *The Embezzler,* his reputation as novelist might conceivably be stronger than it has since become. With the current resurgence of interest in his work, however, it is to be hoped that future generations of readers, yet unborn as early as 1966, will come to understand the twists and turns of recent American history through the eyes of "our man on Wall Street," at his best a truly great novelist with an unsurpassed talent for reducing imponderable bureaucratic mysteries to comprehensibly human dimensions.

Notes and References

Chapter One

1. The full text of Auchincloss's article on Marquand and O'Hara is reprinted in *Reflections of a Jacobite,* 1961.

2. Lionel Trilling, *The Liberal Imagination,* 1950, 200–201; cited in James W. Tuttleton, *The Novel of Manners in America* (Chapel Hill: University of North Carolina Press, 1972) 8.

3. Tuttleton, 248–49.

Chapter Two

1. *A Writer's Capital* (Minneapolis: University of Minnesota Press, 1974), 13; hereafter cited in the text as *WC* followed by page number.

Chapter Four

1. The two nonfiction quotations in this chapter are drawn from Louis Auchincloss, "A Writer's Use of Fact in Fiction," *Probate Lawyer* 10 (Summer 1984): 1–10.

Chapter Five

1. Rene Girard, *Deceit, Desire and the Novel* (Baltimore: Johns Hopkins University Press, 1965), 73.

2. Ibid., 24.

3. *Reflections of a Jacobite,* 106–7.

Chapter Six

1. *The Injustice Collectors* (Boston: Houghton, Mifflin, 1950), 6.

Chapter Seven

1. *Life, Law and Letters* (Boston: Houghton, Mifflin, 1979), 102.

2. *Reading Henry James* (Minneapolis: University of Minnesota Press), 103.

3. Ibid., 137.

4. *Reflections of a Jacobite,* 64.

5. *False Dawn* (New York: Doubleday, 1984), 16.

6. *False Dawn,* p. 9.

Selected Bibliography

PRIMARY SOURCES

Unless otherwise indicated, the publisher is Houghton, Mifflin of Boston.

1. Novels
The Book Class, 1984.
The Cat and the King, 1981.
The Country Cousin, 1978.
The Dark Lady, 1977.
Diary of a Yuppie, 1986.
The Embezzler, 1966.
Exit Lady Masham, 1983.
The Great World and Timothy Colt, 1956.
Honorable Men, 1985.
The House of Five Talents, 1960.
The House of the Prophet, 1980.
I Come as a Thief, 1972.
The Indifferent Children. New York: Prentice–Hall, 1947.
A Law for the Lion, 1953.
The Partners, 1974.
Portrait in Brownstone, 1962.
Pursuit of the Prodigal, 1959.
The Rector of Justin, 1964.
Sybil, 1951.
Venus in Sparta, 1958.
Watchfires, 1982.
The Winthrop Covenant, 1976.
A World of Profit, 1968.

2. Collected Short Fiction
The Injustice Collectors, 1950.
Narcissa and Other Fables, 1983.
Powers of Attorney, 1963. See also *The Partners*, above.
The Romantic Egoists, 1954.
Second Chance, 1970.
Skinny Island: More Tales of Manhattan, 1987.
Tales of Manhattan, 1967.

3. Essays, Criticism, Belles-Lettres
Edith Wharton. Minneapolis: University of Minnesota Press, 1961.
Edith Wharton—A Woman in Her Time. New York: Viking Press, 1971.
Ellen Glasgow. Minneapolis: University of Minnesota Press, 1964.
False Dawn. New York: Doubleday, 1984.
Henry Adams. Minneapolis: University of Minnesota Press, 1971.
Life, Law and Letters, 1979.
Motiveless Malignity, 1969.
Persons of Consequence: Queen Victoria and her Circle. New York: Random House, 1979.
Pioneers and Caretakers. Minneapolis: University of Minnesota Press, 1965.
Reading Henry James. Minneapolis: University of Minnesota Press, 1975.
Reflections of a Jacobite, 1961.
Richelieu. New York: Viking Press, 1972.
A Writer's Capital. Minneapolis: University of Minnesota Press, 1974.

SECONDARY SOURCES

Bryer, Jackson R. *Louis Auchincloss and His Critics: A Bibliographical Record.* Boston: G.K. Hall & Co., 1977. A comprehensive, annotated bibliography of works by and about Auchincloss, 1931–1976. The earliest primary source listed is a story published at Groton; the latest is *The Winthrop Covenant.* Invaluable to any serious student of Auchincloss and his work, Bryer's volume is especially useful for its annotated listing of reviewers' comments.

Dahl, Christopher C. *Louis Auchincloss.* New York: Ungar, 1986. Published too late to be considered within the text of the present volume, Dahl's is the first book-length study of Auchincloss's work, offering a thoughtful, balanced view of his accomplishments. Of particular interest is Dahl's exposition of "real-life" models/antecedents for characters and incidents in *The Rector of Justin, The House of the Prophet,* and *The Embezzler.*

Milne, Gordon. *The Sense of Society: A History of the American Novel of Manners.* Rutherford, N. J.: Fairleigh Dickinson University Press, 1977. Milne's tenth chapter, devoted entirely to Auchincloss, offers a thoughtful and witty overview of the author's work, with particular emphasis upon characterization and style.

Tuttleton, James W. *The Novel of Manners in America.* Chapel Hill: University of North Carolina Press, 1972. Tuttleton, the first academic critic to deal with Auchincloss and his work, discusses it at length in his penultimate chapter, dealing also with James Gould Cozzens. Following a strict definition of the convention announced in the title, Tuttleton omits discussion of such novels as *The Embezzler* and *The Rector of Justin,* seen as novels of "character," concentrating on *The House of Five Talents* and *Portrait in Brownstone.*

Index

118